Carleton Varney Decorates From A to Z

By the Same Author

You and Your Apartment
The Family Decorates a Home
Decorating for Fun
Carleton Varney's Book of Decorating Ideas
Decorating with Color
Carleton Varney Decorates Windows

Carleton Varney
Decorates From A to Z

AN ENCYCLOPEDIA OF HOME DECORATION

by **CARLETON VARNEY**

Introduction by Paige Rense

Edited by Madeline Rogers

BOBBS-MERRILL

INDIANAPOLIS/NEW YORK

Copyright © 1977 by Carleton Varney

All rights reserved including the right of reproduction
in whole or in part in any form
Published by The Bobbs-Merrill Company, Inc.
Indianapolis/New York

Library of Congress Cataloging in Publication Data

Varney, Carleton.
  Carleton Varney decorates from A to Z.

  1. Varney, Carleton.   2. Interior decoration—
United States.   I. Title.
NK2004.3.V37A43   747.8′83   77-76890
ISBN 0-672-51863-5

Designed by Bernard Schleifer
Manufactured in the United States of America

FIRST PRINTING

For my wife, Suzanne,
and for my sons,
Nicholas, Seamus and Sebastian

ACKNOWLEDGMENTS

I WISH TO THANK Madeline Rogers for her help in editing this book. My sincere appreciation also goes to Ernest Wildner Fox, who worked with me daily and diligently on the drawings, and to Brian Beker, a future journalist, for his editorial assistance.

Frances Oka and Irene Frank are equally remembered by me and thanked for their work. They retyped and retyped and finally after four years, through no fault of theirs, only mine, we delivered the manuscript to the publisher.

INTRODUCTION

As EDITOR-IN-CHIEF of *Architectural Digest,* I travel a lot. Yes, it's
all very heady to sweep through United States and European
capitals in a haze of parties and luncheons with successful,
interesting people. It can also be lonely. Sometimes—not often—
one of those people becomes a friend. Carleton Varney became
my friend.

He lives in New York. I live in Los Angeles. We met in San
Francisco. The event that brought us together was an
international design show. I was seeking new talent for my
magazine. Actually, I'm not sure what Carleton was doing there.
Perhaps it was connected with his syndicated newspaper column,
"Your Family Decorator," which ran in the *San Francisco
Chronicle,* among hundreds of other newspapers throughout the
country. I do know he was making sure that a hotel he had
designed in that city still looked as it did when he completed it.

We agreed to have dinner in the hotel dining room. The
group was small—four or five as I recall. I don't know what I
expected Carleton to be like, but I never expect much from hotel
food. Wrong. The maître d' hovered, the chef beamed, as
Carleton conferred with them, inspiring culinary inventiveness,
inciting them to prepare a riot of taste thrills for the Lady Editor.
They cared not at all about the L.E., but they obviously cared
about Carleton. Everyone does. He expects the best from others
because that's what he gives of himself.

We next met in New York, at a dinner party in the
apartment of our mutual friend, fashion designer Pauline Trigère.
Carleton was, I noted, still wearing a scarf instead of a tie. His
signature. Who could forget a tall teddy bear in a flowing scarf?

This time it was a Trigère scarf, because he's thoughtful. He also likes her scarves. Carleton's wife, Suzanne, was there that first of many evenings. Why is it so unusual to like *both* husband and wife? Usually it's one or the other, or neither. Suzanne is beautiful, intelligent, funny and chic. In spite of all that, I like her.

The next phase of our friendship had a lot to do with airplanes. We flew to Cleveland in a private plane along with another mutual friend, art dealer Harold Reed, to see a residence Carleton had designed. We arrived in Cleveland safely, but leaving was touch and go. Rain poured and the New York airports were stormed in. We all had appointments that evening—especially Harold, who thought he would be celebrating his tenth wedding anniversary in the traditional manner—with his wife. As it turned out, he spent most of the evening with us, as Carleton charmed the reluctant pilots into flying over the Eastern Seaboard searching for a place to land. Finally, Baltimore took us in just as we were running out of wine. Then, a train to New York. More private plane jaunts followed. One to see the Greenbrier Hotel in White Sulphur Springs, which Carleton decorated. We couldn't land there, either, so we returned to New York and spent what was left of the day telling the story to other lost souls lunching at 21. We tried the Greenbrier a few months later. This time the plane carried a precious cargo of Beautiful People. *Women's Wear Daily* would have had to discontinue publication if the plane had crashed.

Between all the flights, lunches and parties, I learned a lot about Carleton, personally and professionally. He has been president of Dorothy Draper and Company since he was twenty-two years old. He is a good businessman, he understands budgets, designs fabrics, wallpaper, interiors for hotels, planes, restaurants, grand houses and small apartments, writes books in addition to his newspaper column. He loves best to be with Suzanne and their three children on their farm in Dutchess County, where, scarf flying, he drives around in a jeep.

Somehow he finds time to read, a habit he picked up when he took his B.A. at Oberlin and his M.A. at New York University. He also attended the University of Madrid, speaks fluent Spanish and passable French. The French has improved recently because he has been working in Paris designing an apartment for industrialist Erol Beker. Erol also has a private plane, which will fly us all to Paris. I don't know what more I will learn about Carleton Varney, but I do know he is warm, sincere, witty and an altogether good person. That's really quite enough, isn't it?

PAIGE RENSE

Los Angeles
March 1977

Carleton Varney Decorates From A to Z

ACCESSORIES

Essential decorative elements that can make or break a room. Never, never think of accessories as extras. To my mind they are every bit as important as the furniture, and when decorating on a budget they can be even more important. I remember my bachelor days when my friends and I often decorated with nothing more than piles of floor pillows, baskets of plants, huge paper-moon lamps, colorful posters and one or two cube tables. I'm not advocating that you be that Spartan, but it illustrates my point that accessories can be the backbone of a room. It also illustrates my belief that accessories needn't be costly. I can't tell you how many "museum quality" knick-knacks I've seen that I wouldn't want in my home. A basket of plants, a dime-store poster or a trio of Mexican tin candlesticks fitted with bright-orange candles are every bit as appealing as many of the priceless antiques I've seen.

When choosing accessories, choose those that provide what your room lacks. If you need color against all those beiges and browns, then select colorful accessories: mat pictures in bright hues, fill an old wooden pail with an arrangement of fresh flowers, toss two or three colorful books or magazines on your cocktail table. Or if your room lacks shine, it needs a set of gleaming andirons at the fireplace, a silver cigarette box on the cocktail table or maybe a tiny mirror cube table next to that lonesome lady's chair in the corner.

ALCOVE

A cozy nook for dining, sleeping or being alone. Sleeping alcoves and dining alcoves are gaining in popularity by the day. Many people are building their own, not so much for practical as for purely decorative reasons. If the idea appeals to you, it's easy enough to have the sleeping, study or hobby alcove you want. One of the easiest ways to create a sleeping alcove is to slip a bed between two floor-to-ceiling bookcases. Or you can place your bed in the center of a wall and hang floor-to-ceiling draperies on either side. (The area behind the draperies is handy for storage.) To make this alcove cozier still, drape the wall behind the bed in matching fabric.

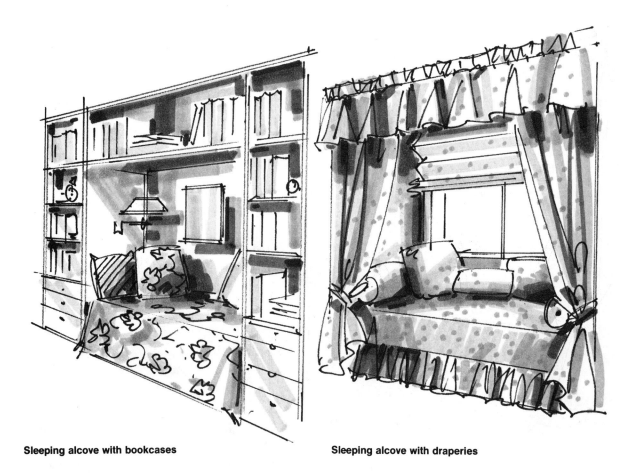

Sleeping alcove with bookcases

Sleeping alcove with draperies

AL FRESCO

The Italian way of saying "out of doors." You often hear people speak of dining al fresco or of the al fresco look of a porch, lanai or sun room. But that al fresco look is much too pretty to be reserved for the porch only. To decorate a bedroom al fresco, paint walls white and the ceiling sky blue. You might sponge fat, puffy white clouds onto the ceiling. Underfoot, lay the thickest grass-green carpet you can find, and upholster the furniture in a summery floral print of red, black and white poppies with green foliage on a white background. You can give walls in any room an al fresco look by painting them a soft pastel shade and overlaying them with white trellis. In a breakfast nook with yellow walls, lay a sky-blue carpet and drape the table in a floor-length skirt of pink, daffodil yellow and cornflower-blue blossoms on a lemon-yellow ground.

Al fresco look

14

AMERICANA

The decorating style that uses materials characteristic of the American civilization. Hurrah for the red, white and blue—these are real Americana colors, and I have decorated many a room with them. Here's a dining-room scheme I like. Paint walls rich Confederate blue and all-trim white. On a dark wood floor, lay a blue-and-white area rug with either a striped or geometric design. The chairs can be covered in red cotton, and for a window treatment try red louver shutters.

Americana is far more to me than red, white and blue. It is nesting tables and Windsor chairs, and it is brick floors, copper kettles, beams and Thanksgiving. Americana is a look I love, especially for country living.

ANTIQUE

Technically, any object that is at least 100 years old. I am an antique-lover, and my country house is full of beautiful old objects—every one of which is used. I have always believed that antiques should be used, while "untouchables" belong in a museum. If you have an antique that's too frail to use—a chair, table or settee—donate it to your local museum and replace it with something you can use and enjoy! If your "untouchable" antique is an accessory, don't hide it in a drawer or in the attic for safekeeping. Put it out on a table or hang it on the wall where you, your family and your guests can admire and enjoy it.

APRICOT

A pale-orange color I often use in my decorating work. Apricot is one of my favorite decorating colors. It goes with every other color, it can be used in every room of the house and it is a color that everybody likes.

Try this color scheme for your living room. Paint walls apricot and all trim white, and paint your ceiling flat lemon yellow. For carpeting, go rich emerald green. Upholstery on your living-room sofa can be a flowery print of apricot, sky blue, orange and emerald green on a white background. Cover your club chairs in emerald green and accent with toss pillows of apricot. Living-room draperies can match the sofa upholstery.

ARCH

A curved structure at the top of a doorway or wall opening. I like arched doorways with arched sets of double doors. And many is the time I have designed bookcases with arched tops; that rounded look is so soft and attractive. An arched top to an étagère and an arched motif on the front of breakfront doors have immediate appeal.

ARCHITECTURAL EFFECT

A decorative afterthought with a built-in look. Today's square, boxy rooms seem to cry out for architectural effects—beams, moldings, mantelpieces and the like. And these days it's so easy to add whatever architectural effects you choose. If you like decorating the country

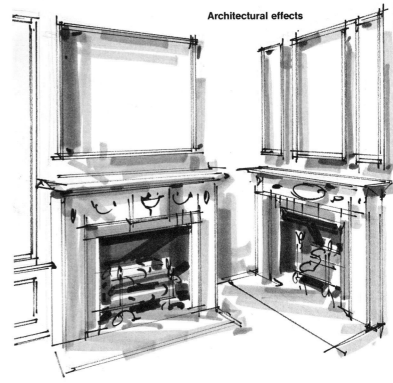

Architectural effects

way, you can put lightweight Polyurethane beams on the ceiling and paint between them with white stucco paint.

If an elegant Louis look is to your liking ask to see decorative wall moldings at your lumberyard. Paint walls French blue and paint those moldings sparkling white. Upholster your sofa and chairs in a pretty pastel floral stripe of French blue and white sprinkled with buds of cosmos pink, daffodil yellow and soft apricot.

ARMCHAIR

A classic, comfortable chair. I am all for armchairs, and I believe they should be used all over the house. I like a dining room with armchairs for everyone. The old way—armchairs for the host and hostess and side chairs for the guests—is not a very hospitable way of entertaining, at least not in this book. Side chairs should be used only where space dictates.

ARMOIRE

The French word for wardrobe. In my opinion, the term "wardrobe" does not do justice to this versatile piece of furniture. Many armoires built today come with hanging space for clothing as well as drawers and cubbyholes, but the armoire—contemporary or antique—can also hold almost anything else you choose to put in it. I have outfitted armoires as bars, and I have used them to house stereos and television sets. If you're a plant lover, why not open the doors of an old armoire, place it near a window and fill it with all your favorite greenery? You can paint its exterior an eye-catching color, and you can paint or mirror the interior. Consider an old armoire for your daughter's room painted strawberry pink and trimmed in bright white. The right side can be used for storing clothing, while the left can be fitted with shelves for a record player and television set. Paint the inside white or paper it in a pretty floral or strawberry print.

AROMA

A pleasant odor. Rooms in the home should not only look pretty—they should smell pretty. Flowers bring lots of fragrance into a home. A vase of lilac can give a room a lovely aroma, and a bowl of floating gardenias on a dining table can give a dinner party a special plus. I love to place a glass bowl of dried English potpourri on a dining-room sideboard, and I often hang fragrant sachet balls in the closets. Scented candles can bring aroma into a room, too. I sometimes light them in our living room before a party. Some people I know perfume a room ever so slightly. A drop or two of one's favorite fragrance is spotted about the room—on the back of a pillow, on the skirt of a chair, on the corner of a rug, on the tie-back of a drapery.

ART

Paintings, drawings, tapestries, sculptures and needlepoint created with skill and inspiration. I like art all over the house. Hang and display the pieces you like and love, but don't turn your walls into a gallery. I like to see a

Armoire

16

little space around pictures. If you have lots of pictures to hang, rotate them. I am all in favor of using children's art to decorate the walls in their rooms.

ART DECO

A fabulous design style of the 1920s and 1930s. Art Deco designers favored certain motifs—the bubble, the zigzag, the lightning bolt. They also liked things on a grand scale. Silver and white were the two most popular "non-colors," along with ebony and coral.

To decorate a bedroom Art Deco style, I would start by painting three walls warm coral, and I would mirror the fourth wall. I picture a thick white shag carpet underfoot and a bed topped with a white satin channel-quilted spread. On mirrored bedside tables, ebony-black lamps with pyramid-shaped shades of white silk would be my choice.

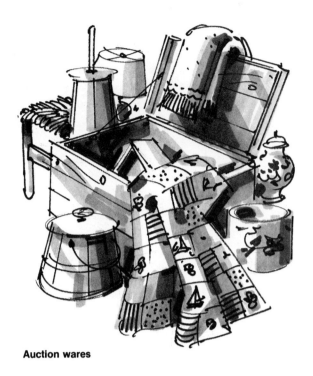

Auction wares

Art Deco

AUCTION

A great place to seek—and find—decorating inspiration. Going to auctions in the city or the country is a favorite weekend activity of the Varney family. We always look for slightly damaged patchwork quilts or torn, faded oriental rugs that can be cut up and sewn into toss pillow covers. An old crockery jug makes a dandy lamp when wired and topped with a pleated parchment shade. I like old round or square wooden boxes; when sanded and stained, they're great for holding flowers or plants. Don't ignore those cartons of old, mismatched china. Slightly cracked odd saucers and plates may not be suitable for table use, but they make lovely wall decorations in a kitchen or dining room.

B

BAKER'S RACKS

Fancy display pieces with shelves generally made of brass, once used to hold and display breads. The baker's rack is a decorating favorite, probably because it is a pretty conversation piece. One placed on a wall in the dining room—its shelves filled with handsome live green plants in cachepots—is a warming note. Or try one in the kitchen, using its shelves to hold cooking utensils and baskets filled with garden vegetables. Or use a small one in the bathroom for storing towels and bathroom accessories.

BALLOON SHADES

A window treatment with a full, puffy look. I like balloon shades because they are casual and simple-looking. When planning your bedroom decor, what about balloon shades at the windows? In our bedroom, my wife and I have balloon shades made from a small yellow, green and melon flower print. The same print is also used on a settee and bench. Other colors in our bedroom are pale yellow for walls, yellow for carpeting, white for trim and white cotton for the canopy bed and bedskirt.

BANDANAS

Those print handkerchiefs of cheery red and snappy navy blue used by railroad men of old. Individual bandana handkerchiefs are being used as pillow covers, or they're being sewn together to make table skirts, place mats, even bedspreads and curtains. And it's now possible to buy bandana print fabrics by the yard, not only in navy or red and white but also in other colors. I like the snappy black and white print for a teenager's bedspread and might mix it with mattress ticking for walls and black and white polka dots for draperies, chair upholstery and bed skirt. For punch I'd add a sprinkling of strawberry-pink and lipstick-red accessories.

BANQUETTE

An upholstered bench built against a wall. The easiest way to create a banquette is to build an oblong box of the desired length out

Banquette

of plywood and place it against the wall. Then let your creativity take over. The do-it-yourselfer can make storage drawers in the banquette; the seamstress can create quilted upholstery covers for it. Those who have carpeting may want to run it right up the sides of the banquette.

I believe in corner banquettes as the perfect seating solution for the small room or one-room apartment. Tucked away in the corner, the arrangement leaves the rest of the room free for other uses. In a small dining room, place an L-shaped banquette and a round table in the corner and turn the rest of the room into a handsome book-lined family room. When company comes, put leaves in the table, pull up a few side chairs and you're ready for a dinner party.

BAR

A necessity in my book. A full-size bar in the home is a luxury for most people; but there are many other kinds that will lend an air of hospitable graciousness to your home without breaking the bank. I often suggest building a bar in an unused hall closet with shelves around the walls and a drop-down shelf that can be lowered across the doorway when the bartender is in. And I love "mini-bars"—an attractive arrangement of crystal decanters (no bottles, please) and goblets on an antique muffin stand, butler's table or lacquered Japanese tray table.

A bachelor apartment I decorated had no room for a full-size bar, but that didn't deter my client. As a successful executive, he entertained frequently and had to have a bar. My solution: a bar and stereo both housed in an antique French armoire.

BASKETS

Today's most exciting and versatile accessory. What will baskets be used for next? I have seen nests of baskets used as stackable storage for sweaters; I have seen needlepointers use covered baskets for stowing their handiwork-in-progress; I have seen a wood-topped picnic basket used as a tiny end table next to a dainty chair. And, of course, I have seen baskets of every description used to hold green plants. As I've shopped the accessory markets year after year, I have seen them grow in importance as an ever more exciting profusion of imports floods in. And designers have started coming up with basket motifs for fabrics, wallcoverings, lamp bases—you name it.

Have you ever seen a hanging lamp shaded with a basket? I saw it recently in a most charming country restaurant where each blue gingham-covered table was illuminated by a lamp shaded with a straw-colored basket. Each table had a basket centerpiece filled with a green growing plant, and a vast collection of baskets was hung on the white stuccoed walls. Doesn't that sound like a charming scheme for your breakfast nook? I would add blue gingham café curtains hung from brass rods and a floor covered with sisal matting.

BEADS

Round, square, rectangular, octagonal or hexagonal elements that some people string and hang around their necks and waists and that other people string and hang as doorways or at windows. If you are the exotic type, you might love a bathroom with a beaded shower curtain and window curtain. Make sure the shower curtain has a plastic liner, and it can be any color, depending on the bead colors. The window curtain needs no liner if your beads are closely hung together. Doorways hung with beaded curtains have been around for many an exotic moon.

For a dining area with a hemp rug and rush-covered walls, what about a natural, woody kind of beaded curtain as a room divider? It can give a kind of flavor to the setting, along with native-looking dining chairs and lots of green plants.

BEAMS

A great way to pep up bland ceilings. Beams used to be necessary structural elements in every house—they held up the ceiling and the roof! Today, unfortunately, most homes come without them, which makes ceilings much less interesting. If you like the look of beams, as I do, by all means have them. There are Polyurethane beams that look like the real thing, or you can scout old barns and country auctions for genuine handhewn ones.

I like beams in a country kitchen, but you can also use them in the bedroom, living room or dining room. In a bedroom designed with the French provinces in mind, I would beam the ceiling and use pretty toile de Jouy paper on the walks and in the areas between the beams. Carry the French feeling onto the bed (a canopied one) by draping it with red and white ticking stripes. And what French bedroom would be complete without an armoire! In this case, one of gleaming wood lined with ticking fabric would be perfect.

BEDS

These days they're almost too pretty to sleep on. There are lots of exciting ways to decorate beds. Recently I've seen a headboard, box spring and mattress all upholstered in quilted poppy-red glazed cotton and topped with a quilted paisley print spread of crisp black and white; a chrome four-poster with a soft chocolate-brown vinyl suede quilted spread against chocolate-brown vinyl suede walls with red lacquered ceiling and trim; a simple padded plywood headboard upholstered in a multicolored floral with matching ruffled pillow shams and blanket cover.

And what about a canopy bed? In years past the term was reserved for beds built to accommodate a tent of fabric, but in my decorating dictionary I have expanded the term to include fabric-draped beds of all kinds. The simplest draped look can be created by hanging two large brass towel rings three feet apart

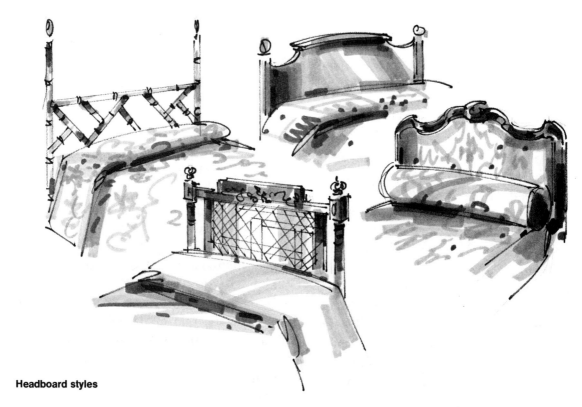

Headboard styles

Canopy beds

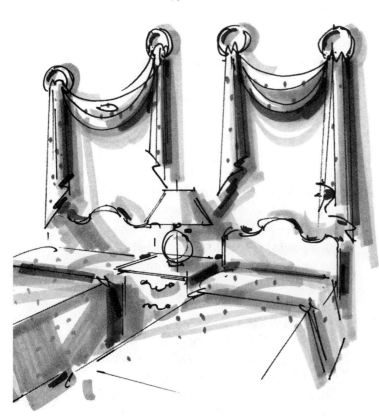

on the headboard wall, one slightly higher than the other, and looping a soft fabric between them.

There are several sizes of beds you can use. King-size beds are the largest, ranging in width from 72 to 78 inches, and, frankly, they are not favorites of mine. They look out of proportion in most of today's bedrooms. If you must have the larger size for comfort, dress it simply; a blanket cover in a pretty cotton print and a host of pillows in pretty cotton shams will do.

I believe that the queen-size bed is today's bed. It is not as wide as a king-size bed, but it is still amply large. When decorating your queen-size bed, try a bed skirt of a pretty green, yellow and melon stripe and a quilted bedspread with an airy, flowery design of yellow daisies entwined in green leaves on a white ground. Your headboard can be upholstered in the stripe to match the bed skirt.

The twin-size bed is half the size of a king-size bed, usually 39″ by 75″. I still believe that the family guest room should house two twin beds with a night table between. Some

22

guest rooms use two double beds in a single room, but I oppose such arrangements. I do not like rooms that look like wall-to-wall bed!

BEIGE

The neutral creamy color that everyone loves so much. I am opposed to rooms that are decorated all in beige; they are so dull. Beige, however, is a great background color for rooms filled with handsome lamps, beautiful pictures and decorative accessories. If a room is decorated all in beige it must be filled with fine wood-framed furniture, a handsome mantelpiece, superb lighting fixtures and lots of color in accessories and paintings. Use beige with apricot and lemon yellow, as a background color with sky blue and coffee bean brown or with strawberry and nasturtium.

Benches

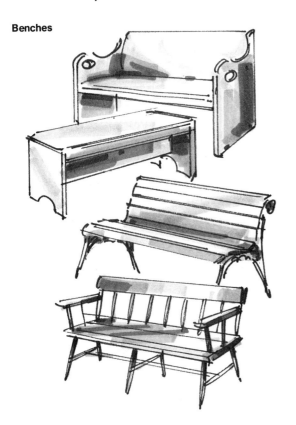

BENCH

A happy alternative to the sofa or chair. When a sofa or chair won't do, think bench. It's a different kind of seating that makes a lot of sense. I would put one in a long hallway—perhaps an old church pew or a narrow, backless bench covered with a long, colorfully upholstered pad. If I found an old ornate wrought-iron park bench in an antique shop, I would paint it white, tie on a pretty pink striped pad and put it in a girl's bedroom. Or I would paint it sunny yellow, top it with a happy daisy print and use it in the breakfast nook.

Bentwood chair

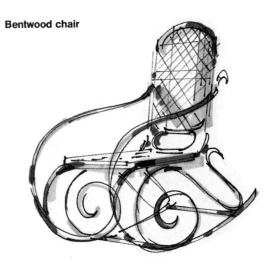

BENTWOOD

Furniture made of gracefully curved wood. It was back in the 1850s in Vienna that Michael Thonet revolutionized the furniture industry by developing a technique for bending wood by steaming and molding it. The all-time favorite bentwood piece is the "ice-cream-parlor chair." In a kitchen or breakfast nook, I would like to see four of these grouped around a circular marble pedestal table. Illuminate the scene with an inexpensive dark-green enameled hanging light fixture. For curtains my choice would be green-and-white gingham café curtains hung from shiny brass poles.

BERGÈRE

A wide, graceful armchair of French design. The bergère chair has been popular ever since it was developed during the reign of Louis XV. Today you can use a bergère with the natural look by stripping and bleaching its wood frame and upholstering the seat and back in leather, suede, wool or canvas. Or you can go space-age by lacquering the frame zingy tomato red, ripe tangerine or shiny ebony and upholstering the seat in patent vinyl. For a pretty, soft look, upholster a white lacquered bergère in a happy floral chintz or lighthearted toile. Or what about the elegant treatment for your bergère: gilded frame with brocade, velvet or satin upholstery.

Bergère chair

BLACK

Every home needs a touch of basic black. People are often surprised when I suggest that black can be mighty handsome. They think of black as depressing, but I think I can convince you that black is as exciting and attractive as any rainbow hue. Picture an entryway with walls of rich coral, woodwork painted white and doors painted shiny black. Or imagine a den with walls of black, woodwork of pickled oak, red tartan upholstery, white draperies and a bright grass-green rug; in my opinion, this room is anything but depressing. If your room needs a dramatic accent, think black: black

ginger-jar lamps in a scheme of browns and beiges; a black lacquered coffee table in a red, white and blue room; black quilted toss pillows on a white sofa.

BLACK AND WHITE

A perennial decorating scheme I never tire of. I have never met a black and white room I didn't like! But I do believe that black and white should always be used with accents of other colors—pick your favorite.

Let's try black and white in a boy's room. I would start off with walls of white, trim painted black and a black and white tweed carpet on the floor. Daybed cover and bolsters covered in black and white glen plaid and fire-engine-red louver shutters at the windows would look super against those white walls. For storage and homework, a handsome white laminated bookcase and desk unit trimmed in red would be my choice; and for upholstery on a comfy chair, try black leather-look vinyl.

BLUE

A color that can be as different as the pale sky or deep water. Blue can be the most difficult color to use in decorating or it can be the easiest. If you are working with greeny blue shades in a room, do not mix them with Wedgwood blues unless you have a floral or geometric print in the same room that combines the two blue tones. When working with an aqua-blue carpet, carefully pick the aqua blues for the upholstery; they should match the carpet as closely as possible.

Sky blue is one of my favorite decorating colors. I consider it a neutral color and use it often. Try a color scheme of sky blue, buttery yellow and chocolate brown in your kitchen, or try a color scheme of sky blue, strawberry, white and apple green in a bedroom.

BOISERIE

The elaborate, carved wood paneling found in elegant French villas and apartments. And, yes, it is expensive. But did you know it is possible to simulate the look of boiserie by installing fancy stock molding right on your plaster walls? To further the illusion you might find an old carved mantelpiece for your fireplace and then paint the whole room a luscious pastel—periwinkle blue or fresh apricot—with those graceful moldings picked up in sparkling white.

BOOKS

A colorful, warming addition to any room, after they are read, of course. Books and bookshelves are very much a part of decorating these days, you know. In my opinion, a wall, corner or table display of books can be just as interesting a part of a room as the colors, fabrics and furniture.

With the fabulous variety of bookshelves available today, it's easy to create practical, attractive book storage plus. In a kitchen, build wall-mounted bookshelves to hold cookbooks and accessories. And under those shelves, mount a wider one for use as a work space or breakfast bar. Picture white laminate shelves against tangerine walls, sunny yellow shelves against sky-blue walls or natural-wood-finish shelves (protected with Polyurethane) against fresh white walls. You can build the same type of arrangement in a bedroom, den or studio apartment to serve as a compact and attractive study.

If you don't want shelves that hang on the walls, think stackables—they're favorites of mine in colors or wood finishes. I recently saw a low arrangement of stackables used to back a living-room sofa. The top of the low shelf arrangement was level with the sofa back and held a reading light and a collection of handsome table sculptures.

Books in entryway

Little-used hallways or entryways are good places for storing books when there's no other space available. You might even turn that neglected hallway into a cozy library.

BRASS

A golden-looking metal that lends lots of warming glow to a room. Brass andirons, brass doorknobs, brass fire dogs, brass-based glass-topped tables, planters, ashtrays, lamps—these are common brass accessories.

I have decorated lots of rooms with brass beds. I like them in rooms that are painted dark colors; forest green is a good background color for brass.

BRICK

A handsome material for walls and floors that's more versatile than ever. Many apartment houses and housing developments now lure occupants by offering the beauty of brick walls and fireplaces. But even if your home is not graced by natural brick, there are alternatives: vinyl brick for floors, brick-look wallpaper and synthetic brick that looks like the real thing and comes in many styles. You can install the quarter-inch-thick fake brick yourself, using a special mastic that squeezes between the bricks to make genuine-looking mortar.

If you are a real brick enthusiast, what about a breakfast room with a brick floor? For walls, choose a fern and basket design wallcovering on a white, washable vinyl ground, and use white cotton curtains at the windows. Breakfast chairs can be natural wood with cane seats and backs; I would have some snappy apple-green canvas cushions made for the seats.

BRIGHTON PAVILION CHAIR

A six- or eight-legged bamboo tub chair. The originals decorated England's Brighton

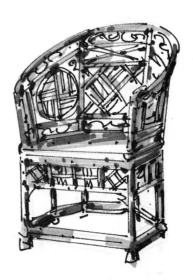

Brighton Pavilion chair

Pavilion, which was built in the nineteenth century by King George IV. I like them around a dining table or flanking a sofa. They look pretty with seat pads of an exotic Indonesian batik.

BROWN

An earth color that I particularly like to use with beige and fire-engine red.

I love brown lacquer walls in a living room with all the woodwork painted beige and the ceiling fire-engine red. On a dark wood-stained living-room floor, lay a brown and white patterned rug. Upholster the sofa in beige suede and cover club chairs in a bright-red leather or tweed. Use glass-top end tables with Chinese tea canister lamps and a shiny brass tray on a wooden base as a coffee table.

BUDGET

An economic factor in decorating. I believe that a home is never finished. Don't start out decorating a home or apartment with the idea that everything has to be done all at once. It doesn't.

Spend wisely!

BUILDING MATERIALS

They're moving from the outdoors in! Have you explored the wonderful world of building materials? I'm talking about siding, bricks, shingles and other materials that are usually associated with a home's exterior but can be used inside, too. If you like the look of wood in a room, why not use natural-wood shingles on one or more of your interior walls? Or what about barn siding?

I would love a wall of silvery barn siding in a boy's bedroom with remaining walls papered in a plaid of tangerine, barn gray and forest green. Pop a forest-green corduroy spread on the bed, a nutmeg carpet on the floor and add some corduroy toss pillows of tangerine, lemon yellow and nutmeg.

BUILT-INS

Furniture elements that are literally part of the woodwork.

There is nothing as elegant as a wall of built-in shelves or cabinets. Yet I rarely advocate built-ins because if you move, you can't take them with you. As an alternative to real built-ins, I often recommend free-standing look-alikes.

In the dining room, I like the built-in look of a corner banquette, which could be constructed of completely portable plywood plat-forms and loose pillows. Built-in bookcases always remind me of a cozy, leathery English library, but if you've priced carpenters lately, you know how expensive they are. The alternative? Free-standing look-alikes. And don't use them only in the den. Try some in the basement playroom, the dining room, the bedroom or even in the kitchen.

BUTCHER PAPER

A homely brown paper product that has moved into a glamorous decorating position. Butcher paper is nothing more than heavy, plain brown wrapping paper. It can be used on walls as is or with colorful designs printed on it. The beauty of butcher paper is that it goes with everything. I like butcher paper for walls and ceiling with trim and doors painted pure shiny white, Chinese red, burgundy or sharp green. I even like it for the walls of a pretty bedroom with white trim, a shaggy white rug, white embroidered curtains and a four-poster bed draped with white eyelet-trimmed embroidery. For the bedspread, I'd try a coverlet of soft lavender and white stripes, scalloped around the edges, and I would add a collection of eyelet-trimmed pillows covered in a small-scale floral of lavender, buttercup yellow, sky blue and white with green foliage.

C

CAMOUFLAGE

The art of concealing the unattractive features of a room. Good decorating often depends as much on playing down the unattractive as it does on flaunting the beautiful. If you've ever seen a beautifully furnished home with peeling walls or splintery floors, you know what I mean. How much more beautiful that home would have been if those walls were papered or camouflaged behind mirror tiles or fabric. How much more attractive that furniture would have looked set on a carpeted or vinyl-tiled floor.

And I'm all for camouflaging unattractive views. If you have a window that looks out on a brick wall or other eyesore, camouflage it behind a handsome array of plants or behind a lovely shoji screen or louvered screen. Or do as a friend of mine did and hang a handsome oil painting right over that window. I would rather gaze at a pretty painting than at a brick wall. Wouldn't you?

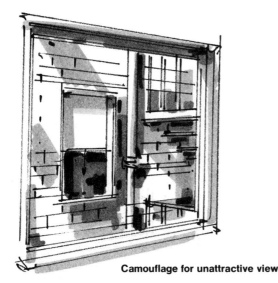

Camouflage for unattractive view

29

CANDLESTICKS

Those accessories made of silver, brass, chrome, glass, etc., that belong all over the house. I love candlesticks and candles. I often place a pair on a coffee table. I use white candles only; colored ones are for holiday parties. And they should be lit only during the dark hours.

Candelabras—candlesticks with two or more arms—can be delightful on a dining-room table, but I don't like them on pianos.

CANE

The beautiful look of woven reeds. I'm crazy about the open, airy look of caned furniture. My office is outfitted with contemporary Breuer-style chairs with cane seats and backs and frames of bleached wood and shiny chrome. But if you really love the cane look, why limit yourself to furniture? There are also cane wallcoverings, fabrics and accessories that give you the look you love.

For a sophisticated bathroom decor, choose a cane-patterned wallcovering in smart black and white. Carpet in emerald green and accent with cinnamon and black towels. The shower curtain can be emerald green. Complete the look with cane accessories: wastebasket, planters for hanging plants and, if there's room, a cane chair.

CANTALOUPE

A fruit color that I love to use with lemon yellow, white and green. One of the prettiest homes I ever decorated had an entryway painted cantaloupe. All the trim was white. The staircase was carpeted in bright grass green, and the windows and bench were decorated with a print of green, lemon and white on a cantaloupe ground.

CANVAS

A hardy fabric I recommend for the home. Canvas is making a colorful showing indoors these days—on walls and tented ceilings, as upholstery and slipcovers, for table skirts and more. I recommend fitted canvas slipcovers in cheery colors for all those hard-use areas of your home: the family room, the kids' room, the living room. Canvas is washable and sturdy, so it can take the patter of little footsteps even when those footsteps march right across the sofa, the chairs and the beds!

CARPET

The world's most versatile floor covering. We live in a carpet century! Carpet goes outdoors as well as indoors and right up the walls, too. If you've never been a carpet fan I bet the new patterned ones could change your mind. I've seen carpets patterned after precious oriental rugs and handmade needlepoint designs. And for modernists, there are scores of eye-catching geometrics in space-age colors.

Carpet is also finding its way into the kitchen, and I'm all for it. For one thing, it makes standing over a hot stove a lot softer underfoot. Carpet for the kitchen should be low-pile for easy clean-ups, and it should have soil-hiding properties. And it should be patterned to help conceal spots.

CARTS

Useful and versatile accessories. With people entertaining indoors, outdoors and in every room of the house, I find the rolling cart an invaluable piece of furniture. Instead of a permanent bar in the family room or living room, I often suggest that a client invest in a rolling cart that can be stocked as a bar and rolled where it's needed. If you have an old tea cart gathering dust in the attic, brush off the cobwebs, oil the wheels and turn it into a pretty plant stand. Or leave a handsome wooden cart right where it is, for use as an unusual end table, buffet server or nightstand.

Cart as plant stand

CASE GOODS

The furniture industry's term for any storage piece, such as chest, armoire, cupboard, desk. Case goods are usually made of wood, but these days they may also be constructed of particle board or molded plastic.

CEILING

A major, often overlooked room area. Why do people lavish attention on their walls, floors, furniture and accessories and put up with boring, uninspired white ceilings? I never do. I believe ceilings should be colorful and handsome. Many is the ceiling I have painted fire-engine red, sky blue, lemon yellow or even black. Many is the ceiling I have mirrored. And many, many ceilings have gotten the trellis treatment from me. A bedroom could have a white ceiling and shiny, brown patent vinyl walls, but why not a peppy, poppy-red ceiling instead? A country-style breakfast nook with wood-paneled walls would look good enough with a plain white ceiling, but it would look super with a ceiling covered in patchwork vinyl.

But ceiling decoration needn't stop with color and paper. It can go on to beams, tents and lattice, too.

And the ceiling is still a great place to hang pots and pans from a decorative wrought-iron pot rack or a section of a wooden

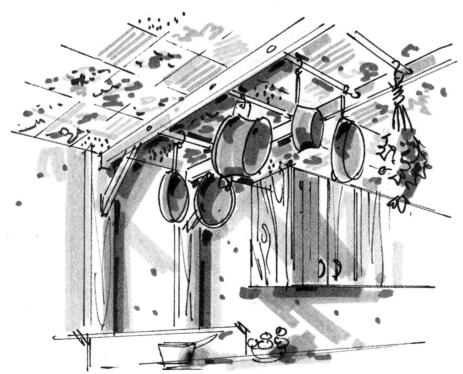

Decorating a ceiling

ladder. Or crisscross your ceiling with natural-wood two-by-fours and use that sturdy lattice-work as a hanger for your pots. As a decorative touch, install plant lights behind the lattice-work and spot green plants and pots of herbs among the pots and pans.

CHAISE LONGUE

A long chair in French. I call the chaise longue one of the greatest furniture inventions ever, and I always try to use one in every decorating job I do. I love a soft, downy chaise longue in the bedroom, but I also love to see one in the living room. If you feel a traditional chaise longue is awkward, create one that "comes apart" by pairing a chair with a matching ottoman.

Chaise longue

CHELSEA FOOT

The upholstered leg. If you're looking for a new sofa or club chairs, consider those that have Chelsea feet. They're all over the market. I like the Chelsea foot on modern or traditional pieces. In a living room I'm decorating now, lounge chairs with Chelsea feet are being covered in a black and white quilted trellis

pattern, and the sofa, also with Chelsea feet, is being covered in a rich apple-green velvet. The pieces will occupy an important place in a room with walls papered in a black and white grass cloth with large flowered areas of melons, apple greens and yellows.

CHENILLE

A charming fabric dotted with pile. Some people think chenille is slightly old-fashioned, but I believe it is very much part of today's fabric scene. At a recent show of the newest in upholstered furniture, what should turn up but white chenille upholstery looking right at home on a squared-off Parsons-style sofa! I would use that sofa with lots of bleached country pine for a rustic look or with glass and chrome tables and batik-covered armchairs for a more contemporary look.

In the bedroom, where chenille is most at home, do something different with it. Instead of using it on the bed, try it as a table skirt, as a curtain fabric or even as a wallcovering. Chenille-covered walls may sound strange at first, but it is a mighty handsome look.

CHINESE

A classic look for furnishings and accessories. Chinese furniture, wall coverings and fabrics have been popular ever since the first European trading ship returned from the Orient with its cargo of silks and other treasures. The chinoiserie style became very popular in France in the eighteeth century when artists seeking to please Madame Pompadour, a favorite of Louis XV, created designs based on Chinese motifs for wall panels, screens and the like. The vogue soon spread to the middle classes and has remained a favorite theme right down to the present day.

If you're planning to upholster your sofa or chair soon and want a touch of the Chinese look, consider a solid-color upholstery fabric, quilted in squares. Try lacquer red or Man-

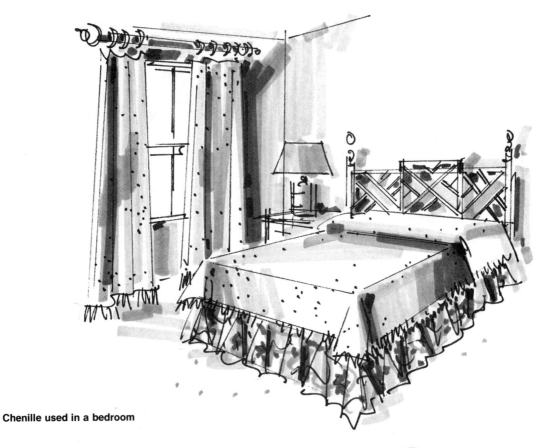

Chenille used in a bedroom

Chinoiserie

darin orange for chairs and sky blue for sofa against walls papered in a Chinese scenic print of sky blue, frosty white and beige with dabs of orange and red.

Many furniture manufacturers are on the trail of the Mandarin look for coffee tables, end tables, dining rooms and bedrooms. Look for one of those big square coffee tables with their simple, elegant straight legs. Or add a little bit of China to your home with a lacquered table or chair. (Lacquer chips, so it is best reserved for pieces that don't get much wear and tear.)

CHINTZ

Once an English exclusive, now a worldwide favorite fabric. Chintz originated in India and was brought to England as early as the thirteenth century where it was an overnight success. These days, chintz is being designed to complement any decor—period or contemporary.

While window shopping recently, I saw a lovely lady's umbrella made of glazed chintz with a tortoise bamboo handle. I liked it so much I was inspired to design a bedroom scheme combining those elements. For walls, a tiny geometric print of soft spring green and white was my choice, with white ceiling and trim. The carpet was pastel-pink plush. For the headboard, bedside table and occasional chair and ottoman, I imagined tortoise bamboo, with the chair seat pad in a pretty pink, white and spring-green floral chintz cover. The bedspread and draperies were of the same print. On a bedside table skirted in pale pink and trimmed in spring green I imagined a white porcelain lamp shaded in the chintz fabric, softly shirred over the shade.

CLOCK

Use one anywhere you need a decorative accessory. If you're looking for a focal point, think clock. A big beautiful grandfather clock

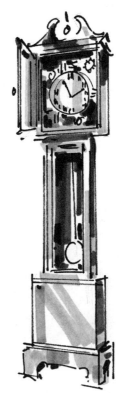

Grandfather clock

can rescue any room that lacks a focal point. And these days you needn't limit yourself to traditional grandfather styles. You can have a chrome-and-glass one or a bleached-wood one. And wouldn't a butcher-block one look super against walls papered in beige and silver foil?

Smaller clocks make beautiful table accessories. I love browsing in antique and junk shops for just the right clock for a particular spot. A recent shopping expedition turned up a tiny silver cube Art Deco clock that I plan to use on a glass-and-chrome bedside table in a man's all-gray bedroom. I also found an old-fashioned brass alarm clock that would look super in a little girl's room done up in ribbons, calico and wicker. And for a lady's bedside table, I suggest an antique gold-filled pocket watch hung on a stand and protected by a clear glass bell.

CLOSETS

They deserve to be decorated, too! Most people never think of enhancing the interiors

Closet with window shade

of their closets with paper, paint or carpeting, but it can make a cheerful difference, particularly in ones that guests see. I remember a hall closet in the home of a friend that was painted cosmos pink inside with a mirror on the door where guests could adjust their make-up, hairdos and hats. What a flattering glow that pink color cast on the faces of visitors!

But why reserve the decorated closet for guests? Wouldn't you enjoy opening your own closet in the morning to be greeted with a happy print of daffodils or daisies or by a bright sky-blue interior? Keep your closets looking neat by concealing shelf clutter behind a window shade. Hang it from the ceiling a few inches behind the closet door and pull it down far enough to cover the shelf and its not-so-decorative contents.

CLUB CHAIR

A piece of furniture that should be comfortable. Do not purchase club chairs for style alone. Always sit in one a couple of times before you purchase it. Every person is of a different size and shape, and there is not a chair on the market that is comfortable to all.

COLLECTIBLE

Any object you love to accumulate. Paperweights, sea shells, glassware, minerals, jewelry—you name it, someone collects it. I would say that collecting is one of America's favorite pastimes. And in my opinion, whatever is collected should be displayed; a collection that is hidden away or scattered here and there cannot be enjoyed by the collector or by his friends and family.

A client of mine had collected antique firearms for many years, but he kept them in drawers, back hallways, trunks, in the attic and the basement. When I planned a den for his new home, my very first suggestion was to use firearms. They were hung on bleached-wood walls, and everything else was left very simple so the collection would really stand out. The floors were stained rich ebony black, the windows were covered with natural beige linen roll-up shades and the upholstery was a flaxen tweed. A handsome room and one dominated by the very personal collection of its owner.

Collectibles

35

COLOR THEME

One way to tie together a small apartment or house. When space is limited, one or two well-chosen colors are better than a rainbow effect. A color theme can be one zingy hue used on all the walls, or it can be shades of that color used in different areas—terra-cotta in the entryway, apricot in the bedroom and a white living room with upholstery and accessories of orange, russet, pomegranate and brown.

Blue-mood people might try deep navy-blue lacquer in the entryway, sky-blue, navy and white batik paper in the bedroom, sky-blue walls in the living room and a sky-blue and white lattice design wallcovering for the kitchen and bath.

CONVERSATION GROUPING

A friendly furniture arrangement. Conversation groupings are easy to plan once you realize they should let people sit comfortably and speak softly to one another. Having the sofa on one side of the room and chairs on the other does not promote conversation. Many times I've told a client to examine the living room after the party is over. If chairs and tables have been rearranged by guests in pursuit of conversation, the hostess has been warned: Her conversation grouping is wrong, and something should be done about it!

Today's most popular conversation grouping is the pit. While I find this arrangement attractive and practical in rooms where one continuous square or circle of seating units takes up less room than the traditional arrangement, I still favor variations on the old theme. I might place two love seats facing each other across a fireplace, with two graceful bergère chairs placed at right angles to them. Or in a large living room I might use two long sofas in the center of the room with a large cocktail table between them and two cushy armchairs forming a "U" at one end. Or I might not have a sofa at all. A conversation grouping can be created with chairs and ottomans alone, but the chairs must be substantial, comfortable armchairs or your living room might end up looking like a doctor's waiting room.

CORNERS

Don't ignore them in your decorating scheme of things! Corners are as important as any other part of your room, and judging from the wide variety of corner furniture, manufacturers think so, too. I have seen corner chairs, cupboards, baker's racks, shelves and etagères in every style imaginable. And corner furniture is just what the architect ordered to provide out-of-the-way storage in today's smaller rooms.

Conversation groupings

Corner cabinets in dining room

If your Early American dining room lacks storage space, a corner cabinet is just the thing. Paint it and the rest of your room restful steel blue, a favorite colonial color. Line the interior of your cupboard with a small-scale documentary print in shades of brick red, steel blue and cream, and use the print for tie-back draperies, too. I would use a pine table and pine ladder-back chairs topped with pads of brick-red homespun. And make sure you fill the corner cupboard with your prettiest china or with a collection of pewter plates, mugs and candlesticks.

COUNTRY LOOK

A way to go back to the land. The country look is everybody's favorite these days, perhaps because it goes so well with today's casual way of living, or because it's part of our nostalgia for our country's early days. Those were the times when unpainted wood, stone and natural fibers were the only materials available.

Today, these naturals are still with us, but so are some incredibly lifelike synthetics. I have seen synthetic carpets that look like freshly sheared sheep's wool, and I've seen synthetic brick that looked as if it came right out of a kiln. And how about some of the synthetic wood paneling on the market? You would have to be a lumberjack to tell it from the real thing. All these synthetics and their natural counterparts are part of the country look, along with barn siding, patchwork, hooked rugs and calico.

A bathroom I recently decorated certainly has the country flair. The walls are bleached wood paneling, and the floor is covered with a beige nylon carpet. The tub is a white, old-fashioned cast-iron model with decorative legs that lift it high off the floor. The ceiling is papered in a patchwork print of bright primary colors.

CRANBERRY

A luscious color on the Thanksgiving table and in the decorating scheme of things. I like cranberry—that tangy red color that can liven up so many drab rooms—with blues, greens and beiges. If you have olive-green carpeting and olive-green upholstery and want to use cranberry, you can paint the walls pale, pale celadon green and all trim and doors creamy white. At windows, hang floral draperies of cranberry, buttercup yellow and powder pink on a celadon ground. Scatter toss pillows of powder pink, cranberry and sunny yellow on your olive sofa. Lacquer an end table cranberry. And if you still haven't had your fill, upholster seats of occasional chairs in shiny cranberry-colored patent vinyl.

CRIB

A bed used by the baby for a few years. Don't spend lots of money on a crib set that will eventually find its way to the attic or basement. Buy the simplest, most durable crib on the market, and decorate it with the prettiest blankets and pillowcases you can find.

CURTAINS (OR DRAPERIES)

Window hangings that are sometimes erroneously called "drapes." Away with the heavy look of windows smothered in yards of fabric. I'm not one of the decorating fraternity who believes that draperies should be totally abolished—just pared down. I'm all for floor-length draperies made to look like café curtains with pretty scalloped or shirred tops.

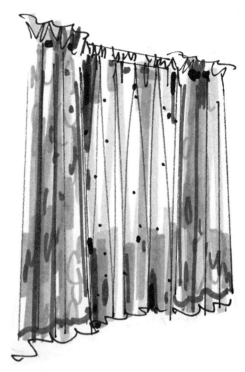

Curtains with undercurtains

And I'm all for tie-back draperies, particularly when they're lined with a pretty, contrasting fabric—lemon-yellow draperies lined with soft sky blue, or chocolate-brown draperies backed with lipstick red. I'm not for draperies that camouflage an architecturally interesting window or a beautiful view. Nor do I like voluminous draperies that dwarf the proportions of smaller rooms.

Undercurtains—sheer, translucent curtains behind the draperies—are excellent for softening the look of windows, closing out unsightly light and yet letting it filter in at the same time. I like white undercurtains only.

D

DADO

The lower portion of a wall. The dado look we are most familiar with is wainscoting—those narrow wood slats that used to be the feature of every home. But dados don't have to be made of wood. I've seen them made of ceramic tile, barn siding, pegboard, and I've even seen them created by simply painting the upper and lower portions of a wall two different colors and separating the colors with decorative molding. I like to make dados by painting the lower half of the wall and papering the upper half. This treatment can be used anywhere from an Early American dining room to a sleek contemporary family room.

DAY BED

A lounging piece halfway between a sofa and a bed. Day beds—or studio couches, as they are sometimes called—are popular because they are so versatile. They can be used for sitting, reclining or sleeping. They are often relegated to guest rooms or family rooms, where they're used in place of tradi-

Dado

39

tional sofas or beds, but I like them in the living room, too.

In a handsome modern living room, I picture a sofa and chair grouping upholstered in a rich paisley of burgundy, poppy and forest green. And to supplement that grouping, I would like to see two chrome-legged day beds covered in tufted forest-green suede. The walls should be lacquered poppy red.

DECORATING NO-NO'S

The things that just can't be done, in my book anyway.

1. I dislike any lampshade that is arranged with drop crystal prisms.

2. I would place all blow-up furniture in the swimming pool.

3. Flower pots must always be clay color —never painted.

4. I do not like round and heart-shaped beds.

5. Danish modern furnishings should be the originals—or forget it. The designs have been badly and cheaply copied.

6. Mediterranean furnishings for living rooms covered in crushed velvets, not for me.

7. Woodwork and doors painted flashing colors such as orange, shocking pink and parrot green are disastrous. Woodwork should be painted simply.

8. Plastic flowers are unoriginal, not pretty. Leave plastic flowers on the shelves of the dime store.

9. His and her recliner chairs in any one room are too much. Generally his and her recliner chairs are unattractive anyway!

10. Never paper the area below the chair back with the same wallcovering that is above the chair rail.

DECOUPAGE

The cutting and pasting craft that's great for decorating furniture, lamps, accessories— you name it! Decoupage involves taking a picture—an old print, a map, a book or magazine illustration—and gluing it to the object you want to decorate. This might be an old marred tabletop or a plywood cube. Or you might decoupage a set of small plywood boxes and use them to store odds and ends on a desktop or dresser.

Add a pretty touch to an Early American dining room with decoupage on the backs of ladder-back chairs. Stain the wood a dark shade, and glue on your design—a wildflower pattern or an American eagle. After the glue dries, protect your design with several layers of clear lacquer.

DENIM

America's favorite fabric for wearing and decorating. Decorative uses for denim are being invented every day. I have seen denim upholstery, denim bedspreads, denim window shades—even a whole wall covered with yards of blue denim used as a giant bulletin board where photographs, citations, postcards, messages and so forth were hung.

I know many a teenager who could use a wall-sized denim bulletin board, don't you? Along with that denim wall I would use a tailored denim bedspread, too. And what about papering the three remaining walls in a polka-dot print of navy, lipstick red, sunny yellow and white? Carpet in sunny yellow shag and hang draperies of denim at windows, over red lacquered louver shutters.

DESERT LOOK

Another side of the natural look. If you think the desert is nothing more than miles of drab blowing sand, think again. The desert is a colorful place, filled with inspiration for the decorator. On a recent trip to the Southwest I saw sand beige, of course, but I also saw rust, delicate salmon pink, soft cactus green. And topping many of the cacti were flowers in vibrant reds, yellows and oranges.

Day beds

Decorating no-no's

Desert look

Desk as night table

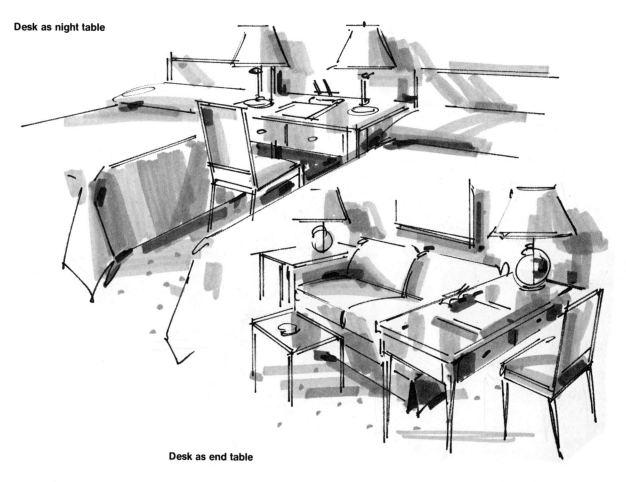

Desk as end table

A desert color scheme for family room could easily incorporate all these colors. Start with a neutral background of sand beige for walls and carpet, and paint the trim white. Continue the neutral theme by upholstering sofa and chairs to match walls. Accent the sofa with toss cushions of soft, silvery sagebrush green and cactus-flower red. End tables and storage wall units can be pale bleached pine, oak or ash. For draperies, my choice would be a nubby cotton in silvery green hung from poles and rings of pale bleached wood. Lighting can come from natural terra-cotta lamps. And what desert room would be complete without pots and pots of cacti?

DESK

One of the most versatile pieces of furniture you can own. I believe that desks can be used in every room of the house. In one of my decorating projects I placed a desk between two twin beds, where it could be used as a dressing table, a writing table and a night table. I often place a desk at the end of a sofa, where it can do double duty as an end table. Or I might place a small desk behind a sofa that is sitting at a right angle to a fireplace.

DETAILS

Little things that can make a big difference in a room. Stunning furniture and beautiful wallcoverings and fabrics do not make a room all by themselves—you need the right details to give a room style. I'm talking about the doorknobs, the switch plates, the curtain hardware and accessories. Picture a charming French provincial bedroom with great French furniture, a pink-and-blue French-stripe wallcovering and a bed topped with matching fabric. But, alas, there are white metal venetian blinds at the windows and a chromium switch plate and chromium doorknobs. Now, picture that room with soft, full-length white embroidered curtains over

scalloped shades and painted china doorknobs and switch plates.

Or bring a kitchen to life with detail. In a country-style kitchen that's all blue, blue gingham and warm wood, how about a shiny brass push plate for the swinging door, brass poles and rings for the curtains, wicker baskets for storing onions and herbs or a colorful dried-flower arrangement. And please don't forget another important detail—lining for the cupboards. Do them in big blue and white vinyl checks.

DINING TABLE

An important piece of furniture that needn't cost an arm and a leg.

When furnishing a dining room or dining alcove, you certainly won't want to spend your complete budget on the table, although you will want something attractive. Have you thought of using a stock metal restaurant table? They come in all sizes, but a 60″ round is my favorite. Buy the table with a padded top, and skirt the table to the floor. You may want to protect the top with a sheet of glass or with clear lucite place mats.

Room size and shape often dictate the shape of the dining table. Long rectangular rooms seem to call for rectangular ones; square rooms look best with round ones. I prefer round tables, which make conversation easier.

DIRECTOR'S CHAIRS

Wood or metal framed chairs with sling seats and fabric backs. The original director's chair used by the great Hollywood directors on the set was as primitive as the first talkies. And just as Hollywood movies have grown up, so have director's chairs. Today, the original wood-and-canvas director's chair is still a favorite, but now the fashion-conscious decorator can also choose one made of chrome and leather or with bamboo-turned frames or in snappy lacquer colors.

Director's chairs

Dividers

44

I recently bought a lot of director's chairs for a party room I'm designing. The chairs all have bleached-wood frames and natural-canvas seats. They will be teamed with bleached-wood tables. And to enhance those natural tables and chairs, I have specified grass-green walls, a white latticework ceiling and a floor of terra-cotta tiles. It's a pavilion look that could work in your dining room.

DIVIDERS

A great way to conquer space. Readers of my newspaper column often want to know how to divide large spaces into cozy areas for dining, conversation or reading. There are so many ways to divide space, I hardly know where to begin. There are screens, of course, and I think they're super, especially when sheet-mirrored or covered with a wallpaper to match the walls. Bookcase dividers are popular, and if you install them using floor-to-ceiling tension poles, they will be easy to move to another room or to a new home.

Or try an approach that will mark you as an imaginative decorator. In a country kitchen, you can divide the cooking and eating areas with a whitewashed picket fence. Or divide your dining "L" from your living area visually with two Greek-style columns. For a divider in the bedroom, you can use industrial chain. Install a curtain track on your ceiling and attach lengths of shiny chrome or brass chain to the carriers.

DOORS

The stepchildren of most decorating schemes. Judging from the number of plain white doors I've seen, most people don't realize how easy it is to turn a drab door into a delightful one. If your room is wallpapered, you can paper the door too and install an interesting crystal, brass or china doorknob. For added appeal, nail narrow moldings a few inches

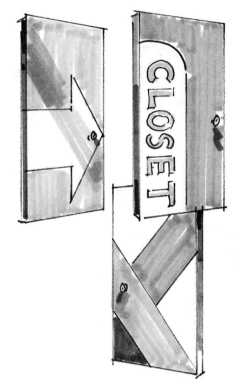

Decorated doors

from the door edges. Wallpaper inside the moldings and paint the door's frame and molding and the room trim in a shade to complement the paper.

In a child's room, liven up that boring door with a supergraphic painted right across the middle of the door, and continue the graphic onto adjoining walls. The design can be as simple as three wide stripes in bold colors—try poppy red, emerald green and rich purple grape.

A soft look in a bedroom is easy to get with fabric-covered walls, but why let the door spoil that pretty soft look? I would cover the door with fabric, too. You can shirr and tack the fabric to the door, or you can stretch it over thin padding.

DOWNLIGHTS

One of today's important lighting techniques. Downlights, usually mounted on the

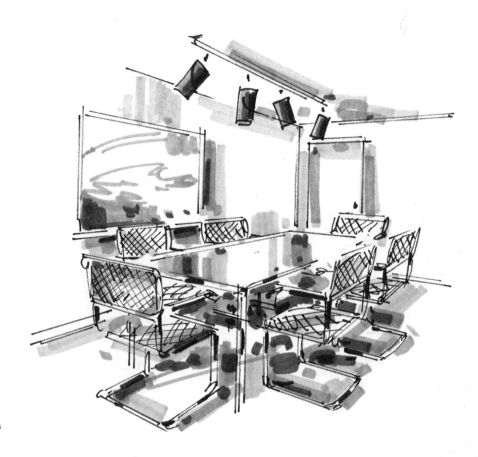

Downlights

Drum table

ceiling on a track or individually, are great for highlighting a particular area of a room or for visually breaking up space. I like the look of a line of downlights in a long hallway. The pools of light formed by the downlights break up the hall's length very effectively.

DRUM TABLE

A round table on a three-footed base, generally with a leather top and a mahogany finish. Because it is so versatile, the drum table is a favorite of mine. I like to use one between a pair of wing chairs in a living-room bay window.

DUST RUFFLES

Fabric skirts around beds, generally shirred. Dust ruffles can be tailored too, with kick-pleated corners. I like shirred and fluffy dust ruffles, generally of a flowered chintz that matches the draperies in a bedroom.

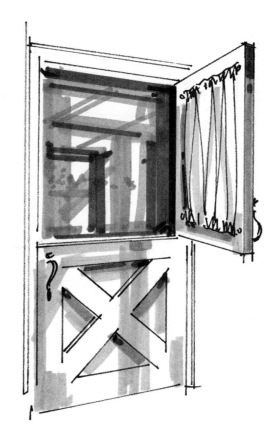

Dutch door

DUTCH DOOR

A door divided in half so that the lower part can be closed while the upper section remains open. I love a Dutch door, and fortunately I have one in my country house. The windows in my Dutch door have a view, so curtaining is not required. But if you need to curtain the upper section of your door, I suggest sheer curtains shirred on a rod, top and bottom.

E

EARTH TONES

Colors found in nature, particularly browns, rusts, blacks and grays. Subtle earth tones are coming on strong, and I'm all for it. They are easy to live with and easy to decorate with, provided you follow a few simple rules. The most important rule is to use earth tones with lots of texture, pattern or sharp color accents.

In an earth-tone bathroom I picture a soft chamois-colored carpet on the floor and a dado papered in tortoise vinyl of the same chamois hue. Above the dado and on the ceiling, sparkling mirror tile would be my choice. Towels would be chamois, rich emerald green and poppy red. The fixtures would be earthy brown, and for the walls in the tub recess, champagne-beige tile.

EASEL

A great decorating accessory. Is there an easel in your life? There are many in mine. A big wooden or metal easel holding a colorful painting accented by a spotlight is a super way to brighten a dull corner of a room. A tiny gilded easel is a pretty way to display a favorite photograph on a night table or to display family photographs on an office desk. And I love to see a tiny easel on an end table holding a miniature painting.

The best part of easel decorating is the flexibility. When you are tired of a particular painting or photograph, just prop another in its place. With an easel you never have to worry about unsightly holes in the wall.

ECLECTIC

A mixture of contemporary and traditional elements. I can still remember the days when a room had to be all Early American or all Louis XVI or all Swedish modern. Today, a room can combine all these things and more. For those of you who yearn for the eclectic look but are stuck with one style, here are some suggestions. If your room is traditional, update it with colors that are clear and bright or neutral. Have the furniture reupholstered in a contemporary fabric; try a bold Scandinavian print on your Louis chairs, a nubby white cotton on your Early American sofa, or a

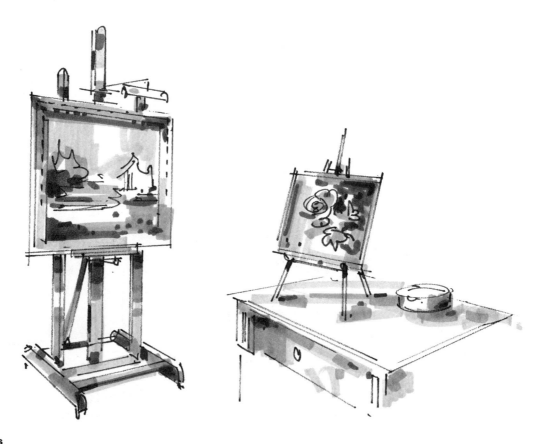

Easels

Eclectic look

batik on your Mediterranean living-room suite. Lighter or painted finishes on traditional pieces will give you an eclectic look, too. For the floors of rooms containing antique or traditional furniture, think of area rugs or sisal matting instead of plush carpeting; at windows choose bamboo roller blinds or vertical blinds instead of heavy drapery. If your room is ultramodern, you can soften the look with oriental scatter rugs, wicker and reed accessories, or oriental lacquered pieces.

EGYPTIAN LOOK

An exotic decorating look that's easy to live with. Does Egypt sound exotic and far away to you? It isn't, as far as decorating is concerned. Many everyday decorating motifs started long ago in the land of the pharaohs. For instance, did you know that the ancient Egyptians were the first to veneer furniture? Other Egyptian legacies—lion's paws, lotus blossoms and the sphinx—are carved on many pieces of European-designed furniture, particulary those of the French Empire period.

Egyptian look

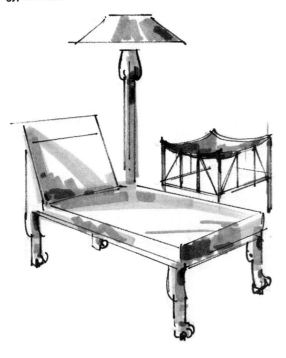

Egypt is also the land of palm trees and shifting sands. It's from those shifting sands that you might get inspiration for a living-room scheme. Start with walls papered in sand-beige grass cloth, and paint the trim rich chocolate brown. Carpet in thick sand-beige shag. Upholster your sofa in sand with chocolate welts, and accent with pillows of Nile blue, pale desert rose and chocolate. At right angles to that sofa I picture two X-shaped chairs. At the windows, hang simple panels of beige fabric trimmed with chocolate-brown gimp. Flank your sofa with a Parsons table lacquered Nile blue, and in front of the sofa place a coffee table of hammered brass. More Egyptian touches: giant palms in raffia baskets and a collection of crystal and onyx obelisks for the coffee table.

EMPIRE

A French decorating style associated with the reign of the Emperor Napoleon. The Empire style (1804-1820) turned to ancient Greece, Rome and Egypt for inspiration. The look in furniture and architecture was square and masculine. Furniture was rarely carved, but it was decorated with a great deal of ormolu. Popular ornaments included the sphinx and obelisk as well as Greek gods, Roman lamps and dancing girls.

END TABLE

The small table that generally sits beside the sofa. I want to rid the world of the idea that end tables have to match or that end tables even have to be tables. I love the look of unmatched tables. One might be a Shaker-style candlestand, the other an acrylic cube or a desk placed at right angles to the sofa. An end table could be a small chest of drawers lacquered a bright color, an antique washstand, a bombe chest, or even a short stepladder. In short, an end table can be almost everything that will hold a lamp and leave room for all the objects you need to have close at hand. When it's time to buy an end table, don't think of looking only at tables!

End table

ENTERTAINING

An informal affair that requires new, more informal decorating arrangements. I say it's time to get out of the formal dinner-party/cocktail-party rut. Many people are entertaining more informally in every room of the house, including the kitchen. One way to break out of the traditional entertaining rut is to change party surroundings or use familiar surroundings in new ways.

Clients of mine had the right idea when they turned an entryway closet into a bar so guests can help themselves to a drink as they arrive. Entryway walls and doors are colored fir-tree green and interior of the closet/bar is the same dramatic hue. Strip lights in the closet provided illumination, and glass shelves mounted on inexpensive brackets hold bottles.

One way to vary the dinner-party routine

is to do away with the traditional dining-room suite of four chairs, table and buffet. A friend of mine did just that. When he and his wife are alone, an L-shaped upholstered banquette and small square table in one corner is their cozy dining spot. If two people come to dinner, two chairs are added, but when there's a larger crowd, folding chairs and tables come out of the closet.

ENTRYWAY

The area in your house where important first impressions are made. I have always believed that the entryway, the introduction to your home, should be as colorful and interesting as it can be. Foyers in today's homes are often small, but that doesn't mean they should be ignored. You can open up the space by choosing an open-design wallcovering such as trellis or fretwork, or by installing sheet mirror on the walls. Add a sparkling crystal chandelier to cast a welcoming light. If you're a book person, you can create a warm, welcoming look by keeping your library in the entryway.

ETAGÈRE

A decorating necessity in these space-conscious times. An etagère beautifully stores your belongings one on top of the other instead of side by side. I use a glass-and-chrome one in my own home to display collectibles, and I know people who use one to hold plants in front of a sunny window. When space is too limited for a large table, did you know that the etagère makes a perfect buffet-style server for parties? Put wine and crystal on the lowest shelf, silver and china on the next, salad and casserole on the second shelf and pretty plants or flowers up top. When the party's over, that etagère can go back to being an everyday storage unit for your china, your books, your plants or whatever.

Etagère

ETHNIC

The look of American Indian designs, Middle Eastern folk art, African inspiration and peasant styles. The ethnic look is already making its mark in the world of fashion and where fashion goes, decorating often follows. I believe a smattering of this look could be mighty attractive and a refreshing change.

Give your living room a touch of the ethnic look by skirting a round end table in an African-inspired print of tangerine, wine, emerald green, black and white. Or hang a colorfully patterned American Indian or Moroccan rug on a wall above a solid-color sofa. The family room can go ethnic easily just by stacking three or four giant batik-covered pillows on the floor, or by putting a North African brass tray in front of the sofa.

Many teenagers would love the ethnic look in their rooms, and here's how I picture that scheme. Walls are covered with Indian print spreads in shades of buff, evergreen and berry red, and the trim is painted berry red, using semi-gloss paint. For carpeting, a neutral

buff-colored shag would be my choice. For the bed, I picture a tailored spread of buff-colored corduroy topped with toss pillows of mirrored Indian fabrics in exotic hues. At windows, I would hang scorched bamboo roller blinds, and I would furnish the room with a mix of scorched bamboo and painted pieces.

Ethnic look

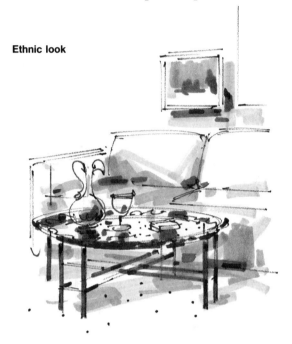

EXTERIOR

It should be kept as pretty as the interior. I love houses that are freshly painted. I love window boxes filled with flowering geraniums and petunias in the summer or with evergreens in the winter. I also like to see a pair of carriage lanterns flanking the entryway, a shiny brass doorknocker and doors painted bright red or yellow or lacquer black.

EYELET

The small hole in lacylike border fabric designed to receive pretty ribbon. Bed pillowcases that have eyelet embroidery borders are a real decorating plus. The eyelet can be laced with whatever color ribbon you choose, and you can change the ribbon as you change the bed decor.

F

FASHION

Something to avoid in decorating. I've never really been a "trendy" decorator, and I'm very glad. I'm delighted I never decorated in the Sixties look of Day-glo painted walls and with zip & zap flashing lights. To me, furniture such as the bean-bag chair and the waterbed are all fashions that are passé. The chrome look in decorating is on its way out, too. Remember, today's fashion can be tomorrow's obsolescence.

FAUX

French for "false" and an important word in the decorator's vocabulary. Today, everyone wants lizard, leather, fur, marble, tortoise—all the exotic naturals—to go with their natural-look decor. But exotic naturals are expensive and the limited supply must be preserved, so decorators are turning to fabulous fakes—and fabulous they are, believe me. There are wallcoverings that look like newly quarried marble, grainy lizard skin or fine leather. There are fake furs for upholstery, bedspreads, rugs and pillows. And if you're handy with a paintbrush, you can make your own faux finishes by copying naturals.

FEDERALIST

The gracious decorating style that flourished in America after the Revolution and into the 1830s. The Revolution caused trendsetters of the time to turn away from British influences and seek a look that would be in keeping with the new political climate. Thomas Jefferson suggested that America model her architecture and interior design on ancient Greece —a great democracy of an earlier age. The Federal period is thus characterized by classical motifs; mantels and doorways, secretary desks and highboys were topped with Greek-style pediments, and furniture designs were graceful and elegantly finished.

If you would like to decorate the Federalist way, you're in luck. Many fine affordable reproductions of Federalist furniture are available. Upholster them in elegant damasks, brocades and satin stripes. Add moldings and architectural details to walls and doorways, and hang swag and jabot draperies at windows.

Federalist style

Filigree

FILIGREE

That openwork design that has a very lacy look. Many is the home in which I have used filigree sliding screens at the living-room windows, often painted white. Filigree has a very Moorish look to me, so I like to use Moorish color schemes—maybe tangy orange, peppery pink, acid green, brassy gold and black—with it.

FINISHES

Wonderful ways to decorate and enliven your furniture. Today, the popularity of natural wood has led us to forget the beauty of other types of finishes. But in my book, painting, lacquering, laminating and gilding are still very important. Some old pieces have great lines but are marred, stained or hewn from dull, uninteresting wood; painting would cover the wood and let the lines show. Or picture red lacquered Chippendale-style chairs around a gleaming walnut dining-room table. The look is traditional, but the red lacquer adds something extra and a great color accent to the room.

FIREPLACES

An important focal point of yesterday and today. If you're a lucky person with a working fireplace, you have a year-round built-in focal point. In winter, those dancing flames draw every eye, and in warmer months, what could be prettier than an arrangement of ferns in clay pots inside your fireplace?

Those people who have no built-in hearth might consider the look of a porcelain stove, potbellied stove or modern free-standing fireplace. I recently saw an old potbellied stove used as the focal point of a London apartment. It had been painted rich royal blue and sat between two windows that were decorated with red, white and beige striped Austrian shades. The walls were lacquered ruby red; and the carpet was a scroll design of ruby red

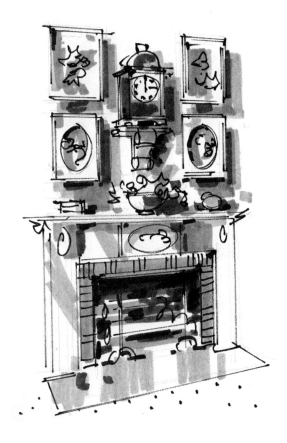

Fireplace

and royal blue. Beige velvet was used as upholstery on a walnut-framed tufted sofa. Club chairs were covered in the stripe of the window shades. And to complete the Victorian look, marble end tables held brass lamps with cranberry-colored glass globes.

FLEXIBLE FURNITURE

Furniture you can use here, there—everywhere! There was a time when bedroom suites were relegated to the bedroom, living-room suites stuck together in the parlor and dining-room furniture never showed its face anywhere but in a dining room. Today that's all changed. Now you can use a small, low chest of drawers as a living-room end table, or you can keep a casual sofa in the kitchen so that guests or family can keep the cook company. And I know many people who tuck a small

refrigerator in the bedroom or family room to hold cold drinks and snacks.

Furniture flexibility makes every room in your home a multipurpose room. You can turn your bedroom into a home office by substituting a convertible sofa for a bed. You can turn your dining room into a part-time office by tucking a secretary desk into the corner.

FLOORS

Not just something to walk on! It's time for pattern, texture and excitement on the floor. There are vinyl floorings that look like pebbles from the Appian Way or like brick or Byzantine mosaics. The carpet industry is coming up with all kinds of patterns for carpets from plaids to geometrics to florals. A black and white checkerboard floor is a decorating classic that can be used in any room and with both modern and traditional furniture. And I have even stenciled a white trellis design onto a green floor in an apartment dining room.

As for texture, there are sculptured shag, velvety pile and nubby Berber-look carpets. And texture is going natural with the look of fiber matting of sisal and coir. Natural fiber matting is suitable for any room of the house and complements any decor. It can be used as is, as a backdrop for oriental rugs or underneath geometric or American Indian rugs.

FLOWERS

I'm a flower decorator, no question about it. I like loose arrangements of garden flowers. I like tulips in country wicker baskets and roses in glass vases. The loose, country-garden look of flower arranging is my favorite.

When the lovely flowers have faded from your garden, please don't think that you must replace those fresh bouquests with plastic ones (the only artificial flowers I like are silk ones). There are other more attractive alternatives. There are dried flowers, dried weeds and

Natural fiber matting on floor

grasses, potted green plants, even fresh fruits and vegetables—all of which make attractive and interesting centerpieces and accessories. One of the prettiest centerpieces I've ever seen was nothing more than fresh lemons and their leaves arranged in a simple white porcelain bowl.

And what about the flowery room? I love a room with walls covered in a green and white stripe and sofas covered in a flowered chintz—big red roses, blue delphinium, yellow daisies entwined in sky-blue ribbons on a white background. And in my flowery room you can be sure the carpet will be Christmas red or Christmas green. The windows will have swags and jabots of the flowered chintz with a sky-blue chintz lining—to match the sky-blue-painted ceiling.

FOCAL POINT

Every room needs one. If the living room of your home or apartment lacks a built-in focal point such as a fireplace or picture window view, don't despair. A focal point can be a beautifully framed mirror or painting or your prized collection of plates, appropriately displayed and lighted. One word of advice: Dominance isn't the only characteristic of a focal point; it must also be beautiful. So when buying a focal point, look for beauty first and size second.

FOLDABLES

The collapsible, storable furniture no home should be without. There was a time when folding furniture was only utilitarian, but today it is beautiful as well as practical and budget-priced. I've seen foldable chairs in every style imaginable, from Victorian to space-age. I've seen rope-seated folding chairs and wood-slat chairs in natural finishes that would be right at home in today's natural-look rooms. And don't overlook the importance of folding beach chairs with colorful canvas slings for children's rooms and even in family rooms.

In a natural-look kitchen, I would team a bleached-wood table with a set of bleached-wood folding chairs. Paint the walls apricot and lay a floor of black and white vinyl tiles. Accessories can be butcher block, wicker and copper.

Foldable chairs

FORMALITY

An elegant look, but one that is compatible with today's lifestyle. Many people avoid

Formal look

the formal look because they associate it with the dark, dreary drawing-room era. That's the last thing I think of when someone tells me to design a formal room. I always start with bright, clear colors and pastels and depend on the furniture, drapery styles and fabrics—elegant prints, velvets, suedes, satins and damasks—to lend a formal air.

In a Georgian-style home I'm decorating right now, the look is formal all the way. For the living room furnished with a mix of antiques and soft down-filled sofas and chairs, I have selected walls of rich pine-needle green with white trim and a petal-pink and white carpet. The sofa will be upholstered in petal-pink linen, the club chairs in soft lemon yellow and the antique French bergère chairs with their dark wood frames in pine-needle green suede. A large-scale botanical cotton print of day lilies, roses, irises and gardenias on a white ground was my choice for draperies, a skirted table and upholstery on two love seats.

FOUR-POSTER

The Early American high-post bed, without a canopy. The four-poster is back in favor —for Early American rooms, to be sure, and also for more modern interiors. I have seen four-posters in traditional carved walnut, maple, pine and mahogany, as well as contemporary versions made of chrome, peeled pine logs and white-painted wood. If you're a traditionalist and you have a gracefully carved four-poster, dress it in frothy white eyelet. Paper walls in an all-over, crewel-look floral of cobalt blue and white. Carpet in cobalt blue and hang white embroidered voile curtains at windows. Decorate walls with gilt-framed family portraits.

FRANCE

A country I often turn to for decorating inspiration. Many people are admirers of French design—French country furniture in particular. It is one of those classic looks that remains in favor because it's so adaptable. I enjoy mixing French country pieces with today's natural look for an effect as informal as today and as elegant as the court of Louis XVI.

Try this scheme in a French country living room. Paper the walls in a small-scale geometric wallcovering of wheat beige, chocolate brown and off-white, and paint trim and ceiling creamy white. Upholster your French bergère chairs in café-au-lait suede cloth and your sofa in off-white linen trimmed with fawn-colored braid. Pile the sofa with toss cushions of wheat beige, café-au-lait and chocolate brown. At windows, hang off-white tieback curtains lined in café-au-lait. Instead of carpeting, cover the floor with beige sisal matting. Accessorize the window area with copper planters and baskets filled with green plants and dried baby's breath.

FRINGE

Trimming for draperies, valances and table skirts that makes all the difference. A fringe on elaborately made valances and draperies is a necessity. I like loose thread fringes on valances and on drapery borders. I like twisted fringes of cotton for trimmings on chair and table skirts.

G

GALLERY

A hallway in a home where pictures and paintings line the walls. Why not turn a long back and black hallway into a picture gallery? Paint the walls white or champagne beige and the ceiling a rich, dark chocolate brown or black. Install down lights on tacks on the ceiling and adjust them to spot on the paintings. Change pictures as often as you like.

GAME TABLE

A sporting decorative accent as well as a practical accessory. Game tables for cards, backgammon, chess and checkers are for everyone to use and admire. I love to use them for playing games and for end tables or accent tables. If a living room is large enough for a game area I always try to include one, complete with a table suitable for the occupant's favorite game. And needlepointers take note: I have seen many kits on the market stamped with backgammon and checkerboard designs that would make colorful and original table-tops.

Gallery

61

Game table

GATE-LEG TABLE

A table with drop leaves supported by movable paired legs. When you swing the legs out from the center section of your gate-leg console table in the foyer, it becomes an oval table that can seat six comfortably at mealtime. It really is a marvelous space saver.

Gate-leg table

GATES

Those outdoor structures of metal and wood that are generally located at entrances to homes. I have always advocated bringing the outside in, and I mean this now about gates. I think a pair of metal filigree gates can divide a living room from a dining-room area very successfully. Single black wrought-iron gates can make interesting headboards in a Spanish-style bedroom. An Early American gate can make an interesting wall decor. And when planning a room divider between your kitchen and breakfast room, what about a white fence with a white garden gate?

GAZEBO

A tiny trellised or screened enclosure, usually placed to capture a lovely garden view.

The gazebo look is coming indoors, thanks to all the people who love garden colors and natural-looking furnishings. For a little of this look in the family room, place a pair of natural wicker chairs near the fireplace. For the seats, make some cushy pads covered with sheeting fabric in a flowered print. If you prefer your wicker painted, go to it, but don't limit yourself to white; go apple green, rich cranberry, cosmos pink or jet black, and always use high-gloss refrigerator enamel for a hard and durable finish.

GEORGIAN

An architectural style that prevailed in England during the reigns of George I, George II, George III and George IV. Georgian decor means large white pediments over doors and large white marble fireplace mantels. And Georgian means brick houses with black shiny doors, big brass andirons and large columns on the fronts of buildings. The decor is very stylish and handsome.

A gate in a kitchen

Gazebo look

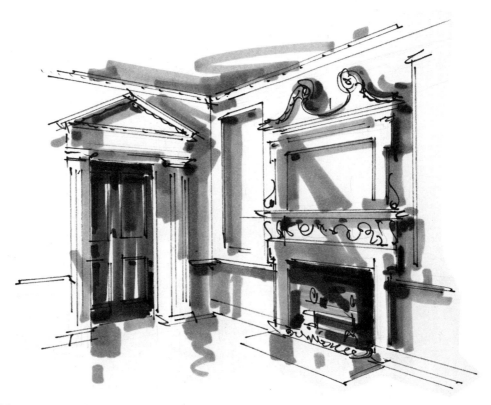

Georgian style

GINGHAM

Country checks with a casual air. Gingham and lace, gingham and ribbons, gingham and eyelet—those are some of the pretty looks you can achieve with gingham checked fabrics in the bedroom, the nursery, the bath and the kitchen. And gingham can take on a tailored look, too. I once saw giant-sized navy blue and white gingham checks used for upholstery and Roman blinds in a man's study. With walls lacquered cranberry red, a carpet of navy and white stripes and rich walnut furniture, the room was handsome, believe me.

GLOW

A rich, warm sensation. I love rooms that have a glow. Try this color scheme in your living room for a warm look: Paint walls soft melon and all trim creamy off-white. For draperies, my suggestion is a yellow, pale-green and sky-blue floral print on a melon background, and they can be lined with yellow. Cover sofas and club chairs in a quilted print to match draperies. The floor can be covered with champagne beige shag carpeting. End-table lamps should be an oriental flowered ginger-jar design, and lamp shades should have a slight melon tint.

GOLD

A precious metal and a precious decorating color. Everyone is gold-crazy these days, but people often tell me their gold rooms are drab or lack zest. In most cases the problem isn't the gold color itself but the other colors in the room—olive green, avocado, browned-out orange and beige. If you love the rich look of gold, use it with flair and always with peppy colors—lipstick red, rich chocolate brown, true orange-peel orange, grass green, Siamese pink,

The formal look is for people with a formal lifestyle. *(see Formality)*

Canopy beds are an affordable luxury. *(see Beds)*

Wicker, especially when it's painted white, has an airy lo
that says "spring" all year 'round. Here it freshens a c
bedroom. *(see Wicker)*

Pattern-on-pattern is easy to do. Just be sure the patterns relate in color and mood. *(see Pattern-on-pattern)*

Armoires are efficient storage pieces for today's small rooms. *(see Armoire)*

Sea shells and sea-shell colors are an important part of today's natural look. *(see Sea shells)*

In this room inspiration comes from the bazaars of India and the Middle East. *(see Ethnic)*

This men's club look is built around a pair of leather-covered sofas. (*see Leather*)

American Indian arts and crafts blend beautifully with contemporary, eclectic or country styles. This collection of arrowheads is the center of attention in a country-style living room. *(see Ethnic)*

Country-look rooms are for me. This my country dining room with beam ceiling, rush-seated chairs, plaid tabl cloth and blue onion dinnerware. *(s Country look)*

White is always right. You can use it in any style of room. *(see White)*

These beautiful needlepoint pillows, gifts from friends, add a friendly look to this room. *(see Pillows)*

I never overlook ceilings in my decorating work. In this man's bedroom, I added punch to a brown, black and white scheme by painting the ceiling rich ruby red. *(see Ceilings)*

Chintz adds freshness to any room. In this bedroom it's draped on walls for softness. *(see Chintz)*

Stencilled floors are practical and pretty. This trellis border is stencilled on my dining room floor. *(see Floors)*

Books add warmth to any room. *(see Books)*

zesty blues. Played against those colors, the gold in your home will take on a new sparkle.

Here's a living-room color scheme to try. Paint walls gold and all trim white and carpet in gold to match the wall color. Window draperies can be gold and geranium-red flowers entwined with green leaves on a black background. Upholster sofa in gold to match walls and carpeting and put geranium-red and black pillows on it. Club chairs can be covered in a print to match the draperies. End tables can be black with gold trim, and the coffee table can have a brass base and glass top.

GRANDFATHER CLOCK, GRANDMOTHER CLOCK

The grandest clocks in anybody's family. The grandfather is slightly taller than the grandmother, and both clocks have pendulums and stand on the floor. Try a grandfather clock in the entryway, or a grandmother clock in the living room—or you can put your grandparent clocks anywhere and everywhere in your home. There are modern grandfather clocks made of lucite on the market, but they belong in chrome and glass rooms.

GRASS CLOTH

Woven Chinese grass stuck to a paper or silver foil background. Many people think grass cloth is for offices—and many a bank president's executive suite has grass cloth on the walls above a wood-paneled dado—but it is also for the home. Soft peach over a beige paper ground can be used in the master bedroom. Green grass over red paper can be used on the walls of the family room. And what about white grass on silver for the walls in the powder room?

GRASS GREEN

A color that really brings the country look inside. Try this scheme in a family room. Use grass-green vinyl tiles on the floor, and cover walls with a grass-green, yellow and vibrant red plaid. Upholster sofa in vibrant red Naugahyde and cover club chairs in a grass-green and black tweed. Accent the walls with brass lamps with black opaque shades. The furniture can be heavy oak.

GRAY

A misunderstood color. I love using gray in my decorating work. It is a neutral and can take on many moods, not just the stormy one we usually think of. It can be distinguished as in this dining room: Picture dove-gray walls punctuated with pumpkin draperies lined in sunny yellow, a dove-gray carpet, mahogany chairs with seat pads of sunny yellow and a centerpiece of cheery yellow and orange marigolds in a silver bowl.

A business-executive client asked me to design a soothing apartment for him to come home to after a hard day at the office. I chose beige walls, gray wool upholstery and gray carpeting with accents of shiny chrome, glass and white. At windows, I hung draperies of a modern geometric print in shades of beige and gray.

GREENHOUSE

A garden-fresh decorating look you can have even in the city. Everyone can have a greenhouse atmosphere in at least one room of the house—the family room, for instance. Start by painting walls of woodsy leaf green and the trim white. Paper the ceiling with a sky-blue and white trellis design. Cover sofa and chairs (if they're wicker, so much the better) in a large-scale lush print of vibrant green leaves on a blue-sky background. For occasional tables, my choice would be lacy wrought iron or wicker painted fresh white. Flooring can be natural or vinyl brick. And, of course, no greenhouse would be complete without lots and lots of plants. Have them everywhere!

Greenhouse look

Hang them in baskets from the ceiling and have tall leafy giant tree plants in attractive baskets and cachepots on the floor.

GREENS

The fresh spring and summer color family that I use—and love—all year round. There is nothing as cool and refreshing as a salad of summer greens or a room done up in summery greens—cool cucumber, frosty lettuce green, tangy endive green, rich spinach green. For good accent colors I turn to the vegetable basket; eggplant, carroty orange, tomato red, mushroom are all foolproof choices. And when you use avocado green, make sure there are plenty of those tangy color accents.

GUEST ROOM

A room that should always say "welcome." Be a guest in your own guest room for a night to see if you are as happy as you want your guests to be. Did you sleep well? Did you have everything you needed? If your answers are yes, then your guest-room decorating is on keel. If your answers are no, you have some work to do. I strongly object to so-called guest rooms that are nothing more than receptacles for old, broken-down furniture.

If you put up company on a sleep sofa in a living room or family room, you still must be sure your guest has everything he needs. Is there a good light for bedtime reading? How about some drawer space for the guest to stow clothing? You could place a small dresser next to the sofa, which at other times can be used as an end table. And on that dresser place these additional welcoming touches: a bowl of apples, a stack of fresh towels, a decorative box of facial tissues, a small mirror with stand for the lady guest, a tiny bouquet of flowers or a green plant, an ashtray for the guest who smokes. That's a warm welcome!

66

H

HALL TREES

Those very decorative wrought-iron or wooden umbrella coat and hat stands. Hall trees have a lot of character, and they are as useful as the hall closet. I've painted many a wrought-iron hall tree, some white, others jet black. Wooden hall trees are nice in entryways in country interiors. Some are even outfitted with a bench and mirror.

HALLWAY

Don't overlook its decorating potential. Hallways are as important as the other areas of your home and in many cases as useful. A wide hallway, for instance, can be used to store books on handsome floor-to-ceiling shelves. Shallow louver-door closets built along the length of your hallway can store linens, clothing and sports equipment. Or turn your hallways into a personal art gallery where you display the artistic efforts of family and friends.

If your hallway can be seen from an adjoining room, paint it a rich color keyed to the adjacent room's decor. For example, if your

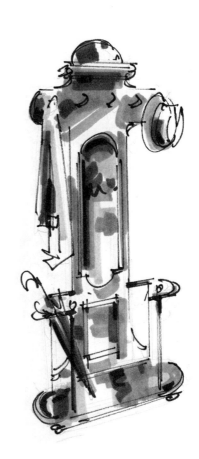

Hall tree

living-room upholstery is rust velvet, paint the hallway rust or cover its walls with a paisley wallcovering of rust, black, emerald green and beige.

HANDCRAFTED LOOK

The look of things handmade. We're living through a crafts explosion; baskets, crochet, macramé, handwoven fabrics, pottery and more are all making the decorating scene. I have seen penthouses and palazzos where handmade baskets and handthrown pottery sit right next to priceless antiques. And I have seen handmade quilts on the walls of country houses, and macramé curtains personalizing the windows of nondescript modern apartments.

And now, manufacturers have started turning out products with a handcrafted look. I have seen fabrics with the look of batik, crewel or needlepoint, ceramic lamps with the look of woven baskets and bedspreads that look like fine crocheted heirlooms.

I discovered recently that the den in Gracie Mansion, the official residence of the mayor of New York, is decorated with crewel. The pattern, flowers of daffodil yellow, petal pink, sky blue and spring greens, is used on fireside wing chairs, on draperies trimmed with deep green fringe and on a tuxedo sofa. The sofa is flanked by two club chairs upholstered in raspberry pink velvet.

HANDKERCHIEF TABLE

A drop-leaf table that can become a square. It is actually a triangle when not fully opened. I've used a handkerchief table in a corner of many a library I've decorated. Its Williamsburg design is very traditional, and it has a great look when one leaf is down.

Handcrafted look

68

HARDWARE

A small decorating detail that can make a big difference. Everyone thinks that hardware is such a little thing, but remember that in decorating little niceties say a great deal. Little things make a difference in a kitchen where a plain white room can be transformed by cupboard pulls of lucite filled with colorful beans, or in a bathroom where brass rings are used to hold towels, or in a wallpapered room that has papered switch plates, too. And little things mean a lot to a front door that has a super handle—a giant brass knob would certainly reflect well on your taste and your hospitality. Or use an old flatiron as a door pull on the door of your country home.

Hardware

HARVEST TABLE

A simple, straight, long table—sometimes made of crude wood—that has drop leaves. The harvest table is part of our American heritage. In early times the pilgrims would gather around it to celebrate the joys of a fine crop. It looks well in the dining room, but it is also very convenient in the foyer of a small apartment, where it can double as a hall console and as a dining table.

HEADBOARD

That great support at the head of your bed. A headboard can be made of just about anything. I've seen cane headboards and upholstered headboards. I've made headboards of picket-fence posts and of old carved doors. I must say I've never enjoyed sleeping in a bed that didn't have a headboard.

HEPPLEWHITE

An eighteenth-century furniture style that is a twentieth-century staple. Hepplewhite furniture, named for its designer George Hepplewhite, is loved for its graceful curves, its shield-back chairs and its classical, restrained carving. Most Hepplewhite originals and many of the reproductions are made of mahogany. I love Hepplewhite shield-back chairs in the dining room. You can use them with a contemporary glass and steel table, a colorful Parsons table or a fine wood Hepplewhite-style mahogany table. If decorating in the traditional manner, use pretty pastels: pineapple-yellow walls, white moldings and doors, seat pads of apricot velvet and draperies in a rich satin stripe of pineapple, apricot and pale powder blue.

HERRINGBONE

A subdued zigzag pattern that has moved from men's suits into the home. Herringbone is one of those go-with-anything patterns that

Hepplewhite style

Herringbone floor

makes a decorator's life a little bit easier. When in doubt about what to use on the chair next to your rust sofa, go herringbone in shades of rust and off-white. When you're looking for a quiet yet exciting wall treatment, choose a herringbone paper of fabric for that wall. It can be used on floors, too. I had a wood parquet floor stained in a alternating zigzags of dark and light stain to create a herringbone pattern, and I've seen herringbone tile floors, too.

HIGH-RISER

Two beds in one and a common replacement for a standard sofa. Today's high-risers, descendents of the trundle bed, have many uses. You find them in children's rooms where the lower bed is reserved for sleep-over friends. Or you find them covered with pillows in family rooms where they are used as budget sofas. And sometimes you see them in living rooms with extra pillows and bolsters for comfortable support.

HOOKED RUG

A rug made by pulling yarn or cloth strips through a tough canvas backing. Hooked rugs and Early American rooms are made for each other. Picture this pretty scene: a pair of cheery red wing chairs sitting by a fireside, with a floral hooked rug of red roses with green foliage on a crisp black background between them.

HOUND'S TOOTH

A check pattern for those who like the tailored look. They don't say "clean as a hound's tooth" for nothing. Hound's tooth—the check, that is—is one of the cleanest-looking designs around for upholstery, draperies and wallcoverings. The tailored look for a bachelor's first apartment might be nothing more than a variation on a hound's-tooth theme.

70

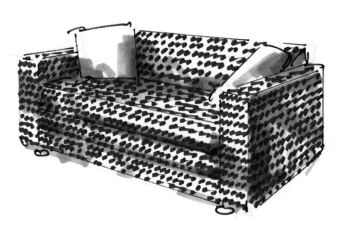

Hound's-tooth upholstery

Hunt table

Dove gray and white hound's-tooth-check paper on walls; gray flannel upholstery on two love seats; black and white tweedy carpeting; and for color, fat toss pillows and draperies of pumpkin-orange velvet. For punch, paint doors pumpkin, trim pure white and the ceiling pale dove gray.

HUNT TABLE

A crescent-shaped table with drop leaves. The crescent-shaped hunt tables are often used today as desks in English-style interiors. They can also be used as long sideboards.

The nicest thing about a hunt table is its height. People can gather around it at a buffet and serve themselves very easily. Hunt boards are hunt tables with drawers, and they are best used in colonial and country rooms.

HURRICANE SHADES

Those tall glass shades that fit over candlesticks. There are hurricane shades for wall sconces and for table candlesticks. I love to see a pair of hurricane shades on a dining table, maybe decorated with ribbons and fir cones at Christmas time for a truly festive look.

I've seen many hurricane shade lamps on the market that have been created for today's modern rooms. Many have bases filled with sea shells or colored sand, and I could see one in a modern beach house. A white accordion-pleated shade would be necessary for the lamp, however.

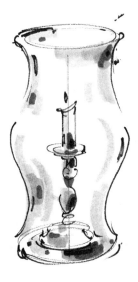

Hurricane shade

71

HUTCH

Storage cupboard with open shelves for display—and open-ended decorating potential! The hutch is one of my favorite members of the cupboard family. Use one in a country kitchen—store pots and pans below and display your pretty serving pieces on top. Use one in the living room as a great bar; store pretty cut-crystal decanters and glassware on the shelves and keep bottles behind closed doors underneath. I even saw a hutch used in a big old-fashioned bathroom. Cosmetics, perfume, bath oils and such went on the shelves, and towels were stored on the bottom.

Hutch

I

IMAGINATION

The most important decorating ingredient. Fifteen years ago some newlywed friends of mine couldn't afford a sofa or even an armchair, so they employed imagination and bought colorful fabric remnants to cover giant floor pillows. Today, as you know, that idea has caught on, and manufacturers now commercially produce pillow furniture.

If wall decoration on a shoestring is your problem, use your imagination and hang an inexpensive rug on the wall, or sketch and frame a colorful swatch of fabric. Walls look handsome hung with arrangements of all kinds of inexpensive objects—decorative combs in the bathroom, interesting copper molds in the kitchen, plates in the dining room. So the next time you reach a decorating dead end, use your imagination.

INDIA

An exotic land bursting with decorating inspiration for America. Indian fabrics, Indian brasses, Indian embroideries, Indian furniture—is there any Indian object that isn't beautiful and decorative? And the best thing about decorating the Indian way is that it's inexpensive. Buy yards and yards of inexpensive Indian cotton fabric in a print of rich golds and browns touched with black and lavish it on walls for a luxurious look. Carpet in chocolate brown, upholster all furniture in brown corduroy and accent with colorful Indian cushions in shades of red.

In a bedroom, hang curtains of crinkly white Indian cotton and cover the bed in an off-white fringed spread of nubby Indian cotton. Paint walls and doors indigo with white woodwork, and lay an exotic Indian carpet in a riot of colors. Top white lacquered end tables with Indian brass lamps, shaded in white.

INDIAN

American Indian, that is, and this look in decorating is here. Copies of original American Indian baskets are everywhere, and many is the Indian rug purchased at auction that now hangs on a family-room wall. American Indian designs are being printed on fabric for bedspreads, draperies and upholstery. I have a collection of forty American Indian spear heads that I have mounted and framed, and it is a conversation piece in my country living room. The great thing about American Indian artifacts is that they look so well in all interiors—modern, country and very French or English traditional settings.

INDIRECT LIGHTING

The kind of lighting everyone wants for illuminating paintings. It is generally a costly proposition but well worth it! Indirect light is actually light from a concealed source. A lighted breakfront that has glass shelves accessorized with beautiful porcelain is handsome to behold in any room of the house. An indirectly lighted bar–breakfront is also popular in American homes. A closet turned into a bar, with indirect lighting, is very appealing.

INDIVIDUALITY

No home should be without this important ingredient. If you have ever seen a department-store model room, you have seen a room that lacks individuality; it is designed to sell furniture. But since your home is not designed to sell furniture, it should display lots of individuality. It should be graced with your favorite colors, and it should reflect your interests. If you love photography, decorate your walls with framed photographs; if you love books, display them in the living room. I would even say that the television can go in the living room, although many decorators would disagree.

INDOOR/OUTDOOR

America's favorite way of decorating. The outdoor look—garden furniture, hammocks, plants and such—has become very much a part of interior design. I've seen a redwood picnic table and bench unit used in a kitchen, teamed with a vinyl wallcovering of a white cloud design on a sky-blue background. For the floor, I would choose a sturdy indoor/outdoor carpet of grass-green tweed, and at windows I'd try grass-green louver shutters.

Give a family room a casual outdoorsy flavor with a hammock of white rope. Installing a hammock indoors is easy, but you must make sure your walls are strong enough to support the weight. Furnish this gardenlike room with vinyl furniture in cheery sunshine yellow or with lacy wrought-iron garden furniture. Cover walls in a fresh green fern pattern on a chalk-white ground, and for a cushy pad on that love seat go geranium pink. Decorate windows with pink-and-white striped awnings. The guests who enter will think they're still in the great outdoors!

INSPIRATION

It's free for the taking! Nature's colors, textures and shapes often inspire schemes: the beige and white of a sea shell with the blue of a summer sky; the rich green of a pine forest with the earthy brown of the forest floor; the delicate pinks and violets of the spring forest flowers. And cityscapes inspire me, too. The steely glint of a city skyline against a pink sunset could become a mirrored dining room with pink ceiling, gray carpeted floor, glass and steel table and coral-pink suede-covered dining chairs. Inspiration is indeed everywhere!

INSULATION

The art of keeping warm in winter and cool in summer. Your air-conditioning and heating systems need your help to operate at peak efficiency. If heat and cold air are escaping from your home, you have to insulate better, and decorating, particularly at windows, can help. According to a study by the Illinois Institute of Technology, window shades can cut the inflow of summer heat and solar radiation by as much as 50 percent, and

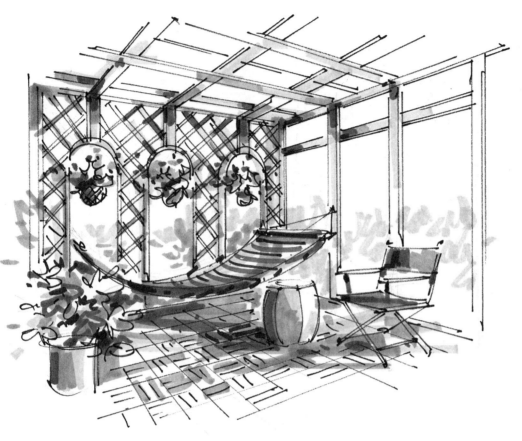

Indoor/outdoor look

can save you money on your cooling bills. There are also insulated drapery liners that will help keep you cooler. And have you seen the Mylar shields that can be applied to windows to keep the sun's burning rays out? I have even seen Mylar window shades that can be raised when sunshine is needed for plants.

IVORY

That creamy-white color. I love creamy ivory walls in a drawing room with a modern rug of ivory and pure white. On sofas upholstered in a nubby ivory and white tweed I would use accent pillows of chocolate brown and deep bottle green.

The room would be furnished with lovely wood-grain antiques, and the draperies would be ivory silk to match the walls.

J

JABOT

A hanging on the left and right sides of a swagged valance. Jabots should always be lined with a pretty fabric. For example, swags and jabots of a flowery yellow, pink and leaf-green design might be lined in a solid leaf green. I also like jabots and swags that are fringed. In a formal living room, jabots and swags of cream beige might be lined in apricot and trimmed in an apricot and beige ball fringe.

JACOBEAN

A heavy furniture style that flourished in seventeenth-century England. Jacobean furniture is heavy and dark—two qualities that should disqualify it for a place in the modern American home. But that's far from the truth. Jacobean furniture styles have never really faded from popularity, maybe because they mix so well with furniture of other periods. I love Jacobean dining chairs with their high carved backs and would love to see them used in a modern dining room with a table of glass and chrome. In that room I would paint walls

Jacobean style

warm mustard gold with white trim and cover the seats of the chairs with a striped fabric of mustard, burgundy and champagne. I'd hang heavy off-white draperies at windows from thick wooden poles and rings. This is a rich look but not an old-fashioned one. When thinking Jacobean colors, by the way, think beige, burgundy, olive green, rich deep blue and mustard gold.

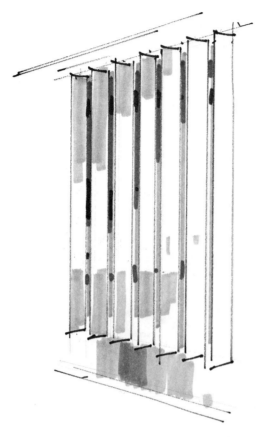

Jalousies

Jardinière

JALOUSIES

Vertical venetian blinds. Jalousies are great in banks, offices and in all those glass edifices. I have often used aluminum ones in modern interiors designed with navy blue, white and lots of chrome and glass furnishings. They are very attractive, simple and practical window treatments.

JARDINIÈRE

A very popular plant stand. For that special corner in the foyer, what about a jardinière? Try one in the living room beside the fireplace or next to the lounge chair in the bedroom. Garden accessories with style belong all over the house.

JEWEL TONES

Rich gem colors for your home. I don't think it's an accident that dark tones for walls are often called by gemlike names—amethyst, emerald, garnet, sapphire, topaz. When you see how a room looks when it's wrapped in a rich color, you'll agree that the room glows as brightly as a jewel.

To see how much sparkling drama dark walls can give, picture a room with no color: sofa is avocado green, chairs are gold, draperies and walls are white. Now picture that room with glowing amethyst walls! And how about some plump toss cushions for the sofa in amethyst, lemon yellow, pale lavender and fresh sky blue?

Or picture this drab scene: sofa is stripes of beige and brown, chairs are solid beige, carpet is brown and walls are blah beige. Why not replace that blah beige on the walls with sparkling garnet? Trim and ceiling can be colored a warm ivory. And how about ivory-painted louver shutters at windows? Sparkle up that sofa with toss cushions in a tiny geometric print of garnet, poppy red and chocolate brown. And I would slipcover those beige chairs in ivory, welted in garnet.

JUNK

A four-letter word, but not a dirty one to decorators. One of my colleagues believes that "one person's junk is someone else's treasure." He really collects junk and uses it in his home. One of his off-the-street finds was a beautiful old wooden mantel with a marble hearthstone that now sits in his apartment. I do not want to imply that you should collect all the discards you find on the street; a certain amount of discretion should be used. Take what you like (staying away from upholstery or mattresses that might harbor unwanted "visitors"), provided the object is in reasonable condition and can be repaired and refinished.

There are many "junk" items that can be turned into treasures. A low three-shelved bookcase that you find covered with peeling self-stick vinyl can be stripped, sanded and repainted. Hang it on the kitchen wall to hold cookbooks or to display your handsome cookware. Lucky is the person who finds junked wooden shutters that can be used to create a hinged screen divider or, if you find enough of

them, to create a paneled dado in the family room.

JUTE

A rugged fiber most commonly used to make burlap. I love jute wallcoverings in natural tones or in bright colors. Choose one for any wall that is badly cracked or marred; its own rough texture will camouflage the damaged wall surface. Try bright red in a small entryway and buy a small remnant of red tartan carpet for the floor. Paint trim white and doors shiny black, and hang a big white glass globe from the ceiling.

Jute

KD

The furniture industry's term for "knock-down" furniture—furniture you buy unassembled and put together yourself. Make sure you buy brand-name KD furniture from a reputable dealer. Some of it is not of the best quality.

KEY PATTERN

A detail I like on bandings and wallpaper borders. I often use a Greek key fabric border on draperies and valances. The key motif is a good trim, and you can find it in a multitude of colors—black on white, red on blue, yellow on green. Wallpaper borders of the key pattern should be used as moldings.

KNIFE BOX

A decorative English box that held the family silver in the eighteenth century. Today the mahogany boxes are often outfitted to hold stationery. I like English knife boxes for decorations. Try a pair on your dining-room buffet for a real eye catcher.

KNOLE SOFA

A popular sofa in today's Mediterranean-decorated rooms. The Knole sofa is practical and has eye appeal. It is an upholstered piece that can be used as a bed when its hinged sides are down. And people love the look of the two looped ropes that hold the sides to the back.

KNOTTY PINE

A rustic softwood used for paneling and furniture. It goes particularly well with Early American furniture. And you can use knotty-pine cube tables with contemporary glass and steel. Blend knotty pine with nubby cotton upholstery and bright batik prints—it should be used with bright, clear colors. Use it all over the house—just don't use it inappropriately. It doesn't belong with elegant French furniture, or with velvet and brocade upholstery or with dark colors.

Greek key pattern

Knotty-pine furniture

Knole sofa

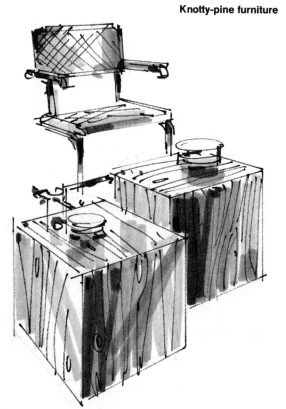

82

L

LACE

A delicate, open-patterned fabric. Lace borders on undercurtains are handsome and favorites of mine. I also like lampshades of lace over cotton—an off-white lace cover over pink cotton lampshade material is very effective. Lace place mats on a lovely polished table top are very elegant. Lace bedspread covers are super in colonial-styled rooms, and lace antimacassars are just right for an old-time 1920s look.

LADDERS

A way to move up—decoratively, that is. If you reserve ladders for utilitarian purposes, you're missing out on a good decorating bet. Have you ever seen a tall ladder used as a towel bar in the bathroom? I have. The ladder went from floor to ceiling and was painted fresh white to blend with the beige-and-white trellis wallcovering. Each member of the family had a different color towel—fire-engine red for Dad, sunshine yellow for Mom, apple green and deep blue for the children.

Ladders can also be used for pretty storage racks. I like to see towels stacked on a Lucite stepladder in the bathroom. Or what about storing your colorful enameled cookware on a stepladder. Or use library steps in any room of the house to hold green plants or sculpture.

A natural-look bedroom for a teenager could feature a fun ladder headboard for the bed. Paint walls white and make the headboard by placing two unpainted ladders floor-to-ceiling at the head of the bed (attaching them firmly to floor and ceiling). Create a permanent backrest by tying a soft foam-filled cushion to a rung of the ladder. Its cover and the bedspread can be washable emerald-green sailcloth. Carpet the room in oatmeal tweed shag. At windows, I would choose natural pine framed shutters lined with emerald-green fabric. Homework, hobbies and books can all be accommodated in a natural-pine wall unit, and to reach the topmost shelves of the unit, install another floor-to-ceiling ladder painted zesty poppy red.

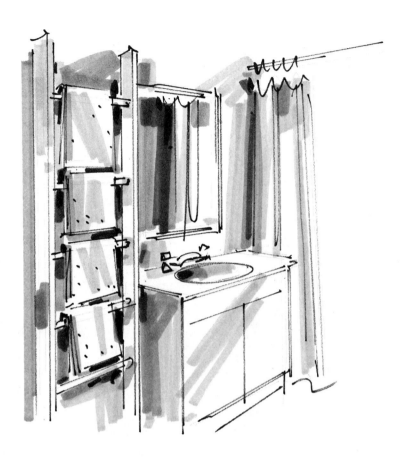

Ladder in the bathroom

Lambrequin

LAMBREQUIN

Another way of saying "valance." If you have a pair of mismatched windows side by side, join them by building a box-shaped lambrequin across the tops of both. Cover the long lambrequin in a fabric of your choice and make draperies to match.

LAMPS

A home's most important accessories. My first words of advice on lamp buying are: Buy a lamp with substance. Ninety percent of rooms across the country have undersized lamps that look unappealing and tip over easily. To give good light there should be about fifty-eight inches from the floor to the top of the lampshade; if it's higher the light will be in your eyes as you sit on the sofa; lower and you

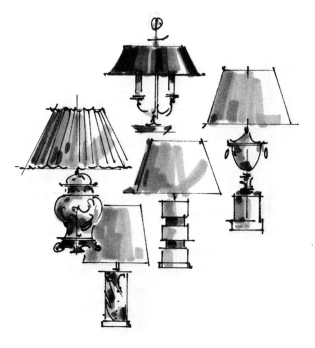

Lamps

Lawson sofa

won't get the light where you need it. I also believe that all lamps in the room should be the same height from the floor and that lamp cords should be as inconspicuous as possible. And you can use anything for a lamp base—old crockery jugs, an old tea canister or even a stack of baskets.

LAVENDER

A versatile hue that goes well with all things. When you want a color that's versatile, think lavender. Although it is usually associated with things old-fashioned and prissy, it is far from that, especially when mixed with other colors. Try lavender with chocolate brown, navy, tangerine, poppy red or with almost any shade of green you can name. Now do you see why lavender should not be relegated to bedroom or bath?

For something different in a kitchen, try a wallcovering of large gingham checks in soft lavender and white. Paint wood trim and doors white. For kitchen table choose a simple white laminated style—a butcher-block model or an

old wooden kitchen table stripped and sealed by you. Chair pads on old-fashioned bentwood chairs can be covered in yellow duck cloth. At windows you can hang either white curtains or curtains made from a floral print of lavender sprigs with green foliage on a white ground.

LAWSON SOFA

The classic of all sofas. A Lawson has a straight, square back and a curved, detailed arm. If you are looking for a sofa that goes with everything, purchase a Lawson. You'll never go wrong!

LAYERING

An exciting way to dress or to decorate. Everyone is dressing the layered way these days, and I've always believed that what works in fashion works in the home. I advocate the layered look of tables with double skirts—a long, solid-colored underskirt with a pretty print thrown over the top or vice versa. And what about the layered look on walls? Paint on

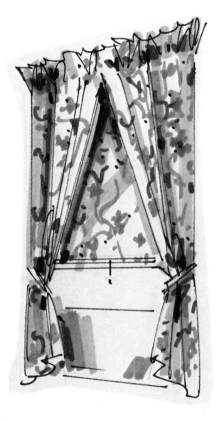

Layering

a color and then wipe over it with a complementary shade. This technique is called strié when done in narrow stripes. And layering is a great look for beds, too. Try it with two prints—a stripe for bedskirt and a floral for bedspread, or a check for the spread and a floral for the skirt. Layering at windows is nothing new; we have the look of draperies over sheers and the look of draperies over blinds. My favorite is the look of draperies over window shades laminated with a fabric that matches or contrasts with the drapery fabric.

LAYOUT

A plan you should prepare to scale when decorating a room. To avoid the juggling-act approach to room furnishing, prepare a layout. Use graph paper, with each block on your graph representing one foot of floor space.

Preparing a layout is not difficult, and it will help you be sure that furniture will fit where you want it to.

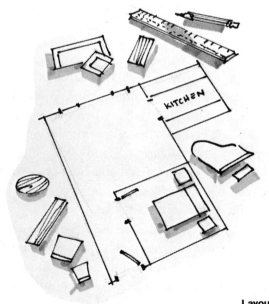

Layout

86

LEATHER

Today's versatile furniture covering for year-round beauty. Do not think that leather means the men's-club look. Today's leathers can be richly colored, but they can also be light and bright—yellows, oranges, apple greens and pinks. I'm not putting down the men's-club look. There is nothing more pleasing to my eye than a beautifully paneled library furnished with deep-green leather-covered sofas, a burgundy leather wing chair and a club chair and ottoman upholstered in a rich red, forest green and royal-blue plaid fabric.

When thinking of leather, however, don't pass up the pastels. Try soft pink leather upholstery on white Louis XVI dining chairs. Paper walls in a silver and pink floral paper above a dado painted soft dove gray. Hang gray moire draperies lined in pink at windows and lay a pastel Aubusson carpet under a polished wood table. Light the scene from above with a crystal chandelier. And for an interesting look in a serving piece, how about covering a Parsons table with leather and finishing the look with silver nailheads? Protect the top of this piece with glass.

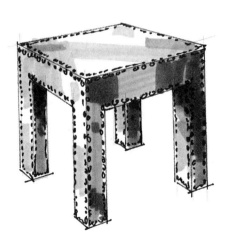

Leather-covered table

LIBERATED DECORATING

A way of decorating that's in tune with today's casual lifestyle. I'm talking about the kind of decorating that is easy to live with and easy to take care of—vinyl-coated wood floors, washable fabrics, comfortable seating pieces. Have you noticed, for instance, the new liberated window treatments? Even the most sumptuous apartments and homes are dispensing with dust-catching draperies in favor of simple roller blinds or venetian blinds. When curtains are used, they are often simple styles made of washable, lightweight fabrics hung from wooden poles for easy removal. Furniture is being liberated, too, with washable laminates, vinyl upholstery and no-mar finishes.

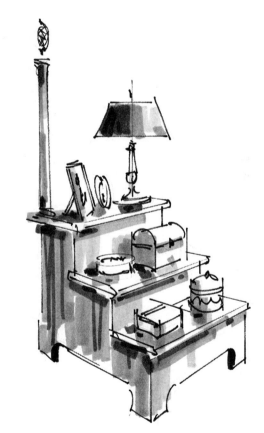

Library steps

LIBRARY STEPS

Those risers that were formerly used as stepping pieces to books high up on the shelves. I've seen library steps concealed in tables and chairs, and I've seen them with handsome turned wooden railings. Today, the library step piece can be used in a decorative fashion. Library step tables are made in lucite, brass and even in mirror.

LIGHT AND AIRY

A look I favor. How can you create a light and airy look when you're stuck with dark, heavy furniture? You can start with walls painted a light, airy color—sky blue, pineapple yellow or apricot—and carpet in the same color. Introduce more light and air with a pretty floral print in pastel hues—a chintz in the living room, dining room or bedroom, or an even lighter, airier voile sheer in the bedroom. Try mixing some of your heavy furniture with wicker, molded plastic or bamboo pieces. And what's wrong with painting a dark, heavy piece that's got you down? Try painting that dark Mediterranean bedroom set a lemony yellow. Paint the walls to match and color the ceiling sky blue. Carpet in grass green and use an airy trellis-floral design fabric in pastel shades at windows and on the bed.

LIGHTING

An important but often overlooked decorative element. I have found that lighting is at the bottom of most people's decorating lists, and what a mistake that is! After all, lighting can affect and even change the colors in your room. It can flatten or highlight the textures of your drapery and upholstery fabrics, or make your beautiful paintings into colorful focal points. It can flatter your guests or make them look pale and sickly.

The one cardinal rule of home lighting is: never, never use fluorescent lights in the home. They don't flatter people, furniture or fabrics and therefore can't be considered decorative in any sense of the word. Lamps and chandeliers are fine, but they must be chosen with

care. Bulbs in the dining-room chandelier should not be so bright that everyone is bathed in harsh light. Put your dining-room chandelier on a rheostat (dimmer), or use wall sconces with low-wattage bulbs and light the table with candlelight—it's still the most flattering light ever invented.

For dramatic effects, I employ track lighting. Installing a ceiling track is not difficult, and once it's up, you can fit it with any number of lights—plant light, spotlights, floodlights—each with a different and exciting effect. Or install individual spotlights to illuminate a painting, a beautiful plant grouping or a lovely window treatment by night.

LIVABLE ROOMS

The goal of all design and decoration. I have always believed that a home should reflect the interests, hobbies and activities of the people who live there, but I have known people to move into homes with living rooms that were too small to accommodate their parties or with huge bedrooms they didn't need. And I have friends who had to pack away their hobbies because there was no room to pursue them in their new home.

Obviously, part of the solution is to choose a residence that has all the features you need to live the way you want to. But if you can't find what you want, you can make a house fit your lifestyle by making the space work for you.

Friends of mine feel that entertaining on a large scale is more important to them than having a large bedroom for themselves, so they turned both the living room and the bedroom of their apartment into sitting rooms for entertaining. They sleep in the dining alcove, which is now a screened-in mini-bedroom complete with a wall of built-in drawers and closets.

Other friends never entertain more than two people at a time, and their house reflects it. Their large living room has been turned into a bedroom with a sleep sofa, and their bedroom is used as a workroom and hobby room where they pursue their interests in writing, sewing and crafts.

I even heard of a family that loved entertaining in the kitchen so much they turned their big living room into a kitchen, complete with wicker sofa and chairs.

LOUIS XIV

An opulent decorating look. Louis XIV, who reigned from 1643 to 1715, is the most famous of the French kings, but the furniture styles that flourished during his reign are not, simply because they were designed on a truly royal scale inappropriate to the way we live today. Many pieces of furniture designed for Versailles were made of precious metals, and the wooden furniture was encrusted with gilded bronze work called ormolu. Fabrics were luxurious, too. Chair cushions were upholstered in tapestry, leather, silks and velvets and were trimmed with fringe or nailheads of solid gold. Wood paneling, called boiserie, was found throughout and can still be seen at Versailles today. The marble floors were covered with thick Aubusson and Savonnerie rugs.

LOUIS XV

A light, comfortable look. Louis XV, the great-grandson of Louis XIV, ruled from 1715 to 1774. His reign is important as a time when interest in decoration spread from the court to the masses. French decorative art became lighter and more graceful. Rooms often curved, and wall panels were oddly shaped. Pretty pastel colors—turquoise, warm beige, pale gold—were popular. Walls were covered with moire, patterned fabrics and mirrors. This was also an age of oriental influences; fabrics were designed à la Turque, with representations of harem ladies and turbaned gents, and Chinese motifs were rendered on fabrics and wallpapers. Flock wallpaper and toile de Jouy were developed.

Furniture was designed for the way people lived. Many of the designs are still favorites today—the chaise longue, the bergère chair, the bombe chest, curved cabriole-style legs. French Provincial furniture had its heyday as country dwellers copied the designs of the court. The country rooms were often dominated by an armoire, and there were lots of rush seats and homespun fabrics.

Louis XIV style

Louis XV style

Louis XVI style

LOUIS XVI

A look that returns to the classics. Louis XVI, who ruled from 1774 to 1792, had a lasting influence on design. His reign is also known as the neoclassic period, since everyone wanted the look of ancient Greece and Rome. Symmetry in furniture design and architecture was revived. Straight lines and Greek ornamentation such as fretwork came back. Furniture had straight legs, often fluted like Greek columns. Much of the French-style furniture being made today is in the Louis XVI style. Upholstery fabrics were plain—striped silks and printed cottons. The French stripe, twined with ribbons and flowers, became popular and is still loved today.

LOUVERS

Those fabulous shutters that always look pretty at windows. Wood-stained louvers work with English library decor; soft creamy beige ones are just right at the windows in a French room. Bright-red-painted louvers go into a boy's room, and yellow-painted ones go well in a kitchen. Louvers go everywhere. They are classic.

LOVE SEAT

A cozy, practical seating piece for today's way of life. The love-seat age is upon us. Many people feel that the three-or four-seater is out because it's too big for today's small rooms. In small living rooms or in one-room apartments, love seats are space savers, and there are many great ways to arrange them. One woman I know "floated" her Tuxedo-style love seat in the middle of her square living room. Behind the love seat she placed a small drop-leaf table where she could write letters or dine. A coffee table in front of the love seat was flanked by two barrel-back chairs. I also like to see two love seats flanking a fireplace.

And what about a love seat in the bed-

Love seats

room? Our neighbors in the country have one upholstered in a ruby-red and white gingham check. Their bedroom carpet is red, and the bedspread, draperies and walls are all covered in a delicate toile design of red and white. Their dust ruffle and café-style undercurtains are also made of the red and white gingham. These same people enjoy love seats so much they have nothing else; in the living room there are two near the fireplace, and the family room sports a leather-covered one that opens up to sleep guests.

91

MACRAMÉ

The art of knotting string, yarn or rope into appealing and useful designs—many of them finding their way into the home.

Macramé done in jute goes well with today's natural look. And I'd like it as a wall-hanging in a Mediterranean-style room with heavy carved furniture. On a polished wood floor I would toss down colorful Moroccan rugs with macramé knotted fringe. And I see a sofa upholstered in eggplant and strewn with cushions of pumpkin, emerald green, ruby red and white. At windows, natural jute macramé hangings and green plants hung from the ceiling with colorful macramé hangers.

MARBLE

An age-old material that is a natural for any room of the house. There is marble for flooring, marble for table tops and even for walls—and I know cooks who swear by marble for rolling out pastry. I'd like to see kitchen countertops in sparkling white marble, which would look super against the dark wood of louver-door cabinets. Combining wood and marble was a favorite trick of the Victorians, and you can still find many fine old pieces—night stands, tables, dressers—of mahogany and marble in antique shops. Try one of those old night stands at the bedside or as an end table in the living room or family room.

MARQUETRY

Beautiful and usually intricate inlays on a veneer surface. I recently used a large coffee table with an absolutely sensuous marquetry top of ivory and teak wood. The border was of ivory linked ovals, with ivory flower and leaf inlays filling the center of the table. It was placed between two sofas upholstered in burgundy wine linen, with sofa pillows of ivory that also matched the carpeting. Walls were all painted teak color, and windows were treated with ivory vertical blinds.

MEDITERRANEAN

A term used to describe furniture styles reminiscent of Spain and Portugal. Actually of African origin, through the Moors, who first

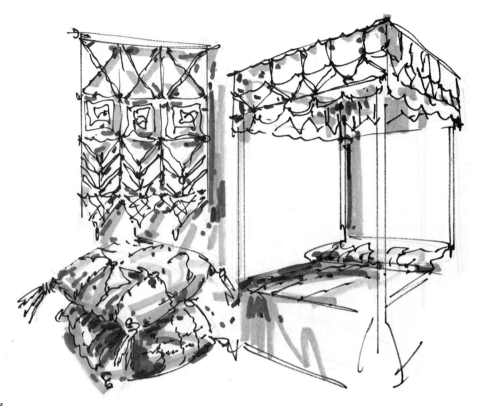

Macramé

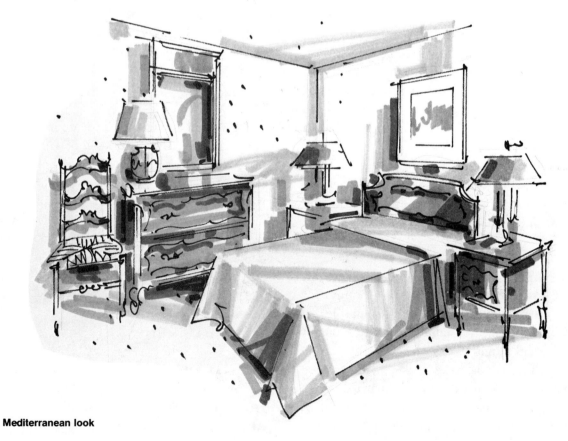

Mediterranean look

introduced it, the Mediterranean look features elaborate geometric designs, deep carving and wrought-iron hardware.

Definitely a rustic look, alas it is often made heavy with velvet upholstery and elaborate swag window treatments. My advice is to lighten up. Paint one or two pieces with shiny white or lemon-yellow lacquer. Replace velvet upholstery with simple washable sailcloth slipcovers in bright, sunny shades—white, yellow, sky blue, grass green, tangerine or scarlet. Lay natural-fiber matting on floors and hang white sailcloth panels at windows, using wrought-iron poles and rings. Choose lamps in the rustic Moorish tradition—chunky brass bases shaded in black or white, or pottery jugs with brown parchment shades. Paint walls white, using stucco or sand paint to give that Spanish grainy texture.

MERCURY GLASS

That silvery, nineteenth-century glass used for bowls, candlesticks, vases, etc. Actually created to compete with silver, mercury glass was double blown and the interior part was covered with silver nitrate, giving the exterior that "look into me and see a pretty face" quality. Try mercury glass accessories on a chrome and glass etagère in a living room with royal-blue walls and white trim and upholstery in a royal-blue and white geometric print. Paint the floor white and accent it with a royal-blue rug. The window treatment can be white vertical blinds.

MÉRIDIENNE

A French sofa of the Empire period. It has one arm higher than the other and most often a heavily carved, scrolly frame. It looks best in light-colored coverings—nice beige silks or pale French blues—and should be placed in the entry of a French-style home.

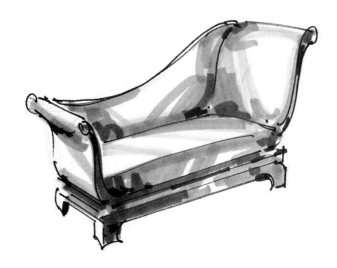

Méridienne

MING

A Chinese dynastic period lasting from 1368 to 1644 and especially noted for beautiful porcelain designs of blue and white. Today I'd like a dining room with a Ming Dynasty look. The upper half of the walls is papered in a Ming patterned paper of blue and white. The dado is Ming blue and the chair rail and all other trim and doors are white. The ceiling is flat white. Underfoot, a blue-and-white area rug in the Chinese manner is laid on a polished wood floor. Draperies, window-seat coverings and chair pads on walnut chairs would have the same Ming print used on the walls. Against the wall I'd place a large walnut breakfront filled with an assortment of Ming porcelain.

MIRROR

A reflection of today's decorating tastes and a beautiful solution to problem rooms.

Since the mirror is one of the greatest ways to create light and space even where both of those qualities are missing, my prescription for many a sick room has been mirrors. I use mirrored walls, mirrored ceilings, mirrored furniture, mirrored window frames—the list is endless—and I prefer clear or smoked mirror in tile or sheet form. Because mirror is unobtrusive, it can be used beautifully with any decorating style from opulent Louis looks to Early American.

MODULAR FURNITURE

Furniture sold in units to put together yourself to suit your needs. Modular furniture comes in many forms, from stacking crates to cushy push-together chair and ottoman units, and pillow furniture that snaps together to make seating of all shapes and sizes. The beauty of modules is their adaptability—you can take a modular bookcase from the studio apartment of your newlywed days and use the same modules horizontally along a nursery wall. Or you can turn your pillow modules from a group of chairs to a bed by night, simply by snapping them together into a bed formation. Though modular furniture is modern, that doesn't mean you can't use it in a traditional room. In a cozy family room, walls can be bottle green with white trim. Sofa and chairs of cushy molded urethane with zip-off covers of white denim can snuggle up to graceful Queen Anne-style tables in bleached wood. And don't forget a wall-to-wall bookcase unit

of modules in a wipable white laminate finish. At windows I would hang simple floor-length draperies of colorful traditional chintz over matchstick roller blinds.

MOIRE

A fabric with a shimmering water-marked design woven in. I love moire for draperies, for upholstery on graceful French-style furniture, and I love the new look of moire in vinyl wallcovering. It's super. I'm using it in an elegant dining room. The walls above a pale-yellow-painted dado will be covered in elephant-gray moire, and draperies will be gray moire, too, with thick golden-yellow fringe. For the seats and backs of Louis XVI chairs, I'm using a golden-yellow with an elephant-gray stripe. And there will be a crystal chandelier above to bring out all the shimmer of the moire fabric.

MORRIS CHAIR

The nineteenth-century chair that was every man's dream. The chair is a comfortable one with a wood frame and loose cushion seat and back. The chair also has a reclining adjust-

Modular furniture

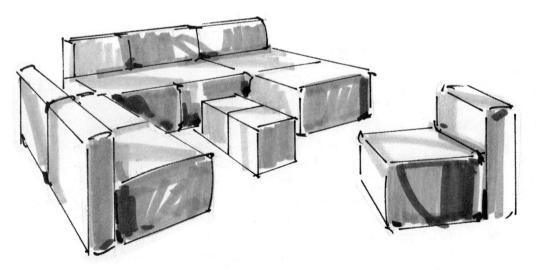

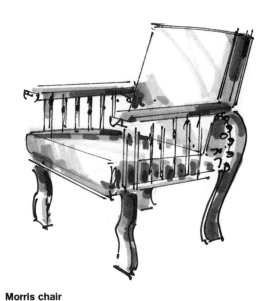

Morris chair

able back. For today's living, I can see the recliner in anyone's library or family room. The cushion seat and back could be covered in any color or fabric.

MOSAIC

A decorative inlay of colorful tiles or stones, used in ancient times for walls and for floors. Now we find the mosaic art limited to table tops, many made from kits, and mounted on wrought-iron legs. I like to see small mosaic occasional tables used as plant stands or end tables with shiny copper lamps in Mediterranean-style rooms.

MUFFIN STAND

A small tiered table used in Victorian days to hold plates generally laden with biscuits and other tea goodies. A wooden muffin stand comes in handy as a simple pull-up table beside a wing chair or at one arm of a camelback sofa. I've also painted them white and used them as plant holders in a garden room. Brass muffin stands with glass tiers make great hors d'oeuvre servers.

MULTILEVEL

Architectural additions—lofts, platforms, sunken conversation pits to give you more living space for your money. Sleeping lofts with storage space, bookshelves or closets below and a bed above are most common, because most ceilings are too low to allow for sitting or walking around. In a high-ceilinged room, a loft for lounging can accommodate bookcases on either side of a foam-slab sofa upholstered in a cheery Scandinavian cotton print fabric. Dining the multilevel way can be done by building a raised dining area at one end of the living room. You can place foam furniture against the "step" formed by the platform, or carpet each area in a different color to create the look of two separate rooms.

MULTIPURPOSE

This should describe every room in your home—particularly these days when space is at a premium. I love a bed/sitting room; a kitchen with breakfast nook; a living room with a game corner and a snack spot. Manufacturers have helped things along by designing all kinds of double-duty decorating pieces—convertible sofas, modular seating units that can be easily rearranged, stacking storage units, expandable tables. But to make a room truly multipurpose, you should also consider the mood, the lighting and the color scheme. A frilly pink guest room certainly won't double comfortably as Dad's study. A bedroom may have to serve as a home office, but just make sure there's adequate light—those bedroom side lamps won't be enough. And make sure that there's storage space to hide your paperwork.

MURAL

A hand-painted or wallpapered scene. I rarely use murals when I decorate private homes. I say this not because I dislike murals

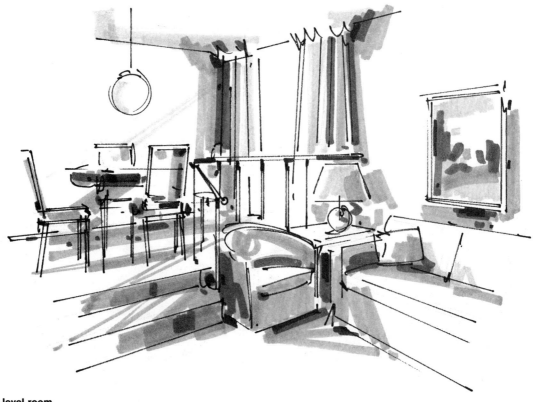

Multi-level room

but because I dislike locking my clients into a look that may become tiring. Hand-painted murals on ceilings and walls are expensive today and cannot be changed so easily.

I like murals painted on folding screens. In our own New York living room my wife and I use a folding hand-painted Zubrer mural screen behind our sofa. If and when we tire of the mural, we can fold it up and put it away.

There are wallpaper murals on the market depicting Mystic Seaport and the Appian Way, and there's that Scenic America mural I love so much. The original Scenic America panels are in the Oval Room of the White House. The reproductions are as beautiful as the originals, and I have often used them.

MURPHY BED

A bed that falls out of a wall cupboard. The Murphy bed is a space saver, and it's comfortable and convenient. It comes in single, double or queen bed sizes that all disappear into handsome cabinet furniture, often with several components—wardrobes, bookcases, desk, filing cabinets and chests. If you want a playroom and a bedroom all in one, consider a Murphy bed unit.

N

NATURAL

A decorating look that's in the news these days. The natural look takes its inspiration from Africa, South America and anywhere in the world where handcrafting is still going strong. It includes nubby, undyed and unbleached fabrics for upholstery and furniture stripped down to its natural beauty. Accessories can be as down to earth as autumn foliage and cattails in a terra-cotta pot. Or why not a bouquet of dried flowers that you pick from your garden and dry yourself? And, of course, live green plants.

For a rustic living room, start by scraping all the dark stain off the floor and bleach it to the lightest wood tone you can get. Scrape paint off wooden window and door frames too—everything has to look bleached and natural. Walls can be stark white, hung with some groupings of primitives, a macramé panel and a bleached wooden mallard duck on a wall bracket. For your floor, choose a beige grass or sisal rug or an Irish Tintawn carpet. At windows, natural rattan roller blinds will go along with some white linen overdraperies.

For this setting I like a heavy woven wicker sofa and club chairs covered in batik upholstery in a combination of russet with magenta, chocolate brown and purple. I'd also like a white linen skirted table holding a wicker lamp and shade. With a natural bleached Parsons card table, use some sturdy old wooden swivel-base office chairs with flat spindlebacks—also scraped and bleached to the lightest shade.

Even lamps can have a natural look: Try a glass oil lantern with an old peach basket lampshade. It looks perfect on a bleached wooden table.

NAUTICAL

A clean, sea-swept decorating look for seafarers or landlubbers. The nautical look is the look of sailcloth, rope, anchors and ships; of snappy blue and crisp white set off by polished brass. There are scores of handsome nautical fabrics on the market these days—prints of sailing ships, anchors, rope and chain.

Recently I used a cotton fabric with a white vertical rope-design stripe on a royal-blue background as draperies for a den and

Natural look

Nautical look

hung them from brass poles and rings. White sailcloth covers two comfy love seats welted in a white rope-style trim. Toss pillows are royal-blue sailcloth trimmed in the white rope. The walls are covered in white sailcloth too and finished with rope at baseboards and in place of crown molding. Window shades are pale-blue linen covered with fishnet. The ceiling is sky blue.

Captain's chairs are lacquered white with seat pads of the blue and white fabric. Bare polished wood planks simulate a ship's scrubbed deck, and tall wooden bookcases hold books, model sailing ships and a brass ship's clock. End tables are brassbound teakwood cubes holding lamps fashioned from a couple of old, squat ship's decanters. As a final touch, the white walls are adorned with international code flags in snappy red, yellow and blue.

NAVY BLUE

A classic color with a sporty look. Navy blue goes with almost any color you can think of, except black, perhaps. I like navy with spring colors—anemone red, daffodil yellow, tulip pink, grass green. I like navy with naturals—sand beige, nutmeg, dark brown. I love navy with red and white, of course. And I believe navy looks best in a sporty, casual or country-style room.

Can you imagine anything more spring-like than a bedroom with walls papered in a floral print of daffodil, anemone red, lime green and white on a navy background? I would paint all trim white, and for carpet I would go natty navy blue. At windows, I envision white shades trimmed in navy and topped with soft, white sheer curtains. Bedspreads would be white with navy-blue welting.

Or why not plan a dramatic dining-room scheme around walls covered in navy-blue patent vinyl? I saw such a room recently and fell in love with it. The table was a traditional mahogany dining table, chairs were Queen Anne style. Chair pads and draperies were a tulip print in yellows, blues, greens and pinks on an anemone-red background. Wall-to-wall carpeting was daffodil yellow.

NEEDLEPOINT

A beautiful craft and a beautiful look for your home. If you enjoy doing needlepoint yourself, I don't have to tell you that the decorating potential of your craft is infinite. There are pillows, of course, but you can also make rugs, wallhangings, chair seat covers— you name it.

Have you seen director's chairs with needlepoint seats and backs? I like those fanciful director's chairs in a child's room with the child's initials worked in bright colors into the chair seat and back. Try navy blue with big red initials on a red-lacquered chair frame.

If you shy away from needlepoint because of the time it takes, try gros point. Because gros point is worked on a canvas with large holes using thick yarn, the work goes quickly. It is suitable for rugs and wallhangings, but an expert tells me it should not be used for items that get heavy use, as it can snag.

NESTING TABLES

Small tables stacked in graduated sizes for a multitude of uses. I have always loved the look of nesting tables at the bedside, next to the living-room sofa or beside the family-room recliner. For the apartment dweller with no formal dining room, how handy they are for serving buffet style. In the family room, how convenient to have one or two sets that can be pulled apart for informal suppers in front of the TV set. You'll find many attractive nesting tables around—in bamboo, wood, metal and molded plastic.

Nesting tables

NICHE

That wall recess where you can display something. Over the years I have found niches a real problem; my clients have never known

101

what to put in them. I do not like a niche filled with a vase of artificial flowers, and I do not like a niche filled with a bust of a stranger. If your home has a niche and you are not using it as the place for the telephone, remember my advice: place into niches only those things you really like. They are always eye catchers.

I like a niche that is painted a contrasting color. If your niche appears in a dining room, what about champagne-beige dining-room walls and the niche painted my favorite sky blue? Fill it with the prettiest in-season flowering plants.

NYLON

The generic term for a protean synthetic chemical that can be made into fibers for just about everything—clothing, fabrics, sheets, carpets. For many years I have used nylon upholstery and carpeting on my decorating projects. Nylon generally means good wearability and practicality, and in today's decorating we are all looking for products of the longest wear and of the brightest beauty.

O

OBJETS D'ART

Beautiful and valuable accessories. I enjoy objets d'art around the house, and I believe ones of the same subject matter should be grouped together in a room. A collection of bird figurines could grace the shelves of a living-room curio cabinet, while a grouping of miniature soldier figurines could be displayed on a coffee table. Several groupings of objets d'art can be used in the same room, but too many of them would be confusing.

OCCASIONAL TABLES

Just about every table in a room—sofa end tables, fret-top pie-crust tables, tea tables, coffee tables, stepladder end tables, tripod cigarette tables, book tables, nesting tables.

All rooms require occasional tables. I like to see a group of nesting tables at one end of a sofa and a round table at the other end. I generally prefer sofa end tables that do not match. No chair in a room should sit alone; it should always be accompanied by some occasional table. What about using a pie-crust table between a pair of wing chairs, or how

Objets d'art

103

about a small book end table as the side companion to a love seat?

When shopping for occasional tables, choose special, attractive pieces. Occasional tables in any room can be of varied finishes, but the styles should relate. A French white-and-gold occasional table would be out of place in a room where other occasional pieces were of the English mahogany and leather vintage.

OFFICE

A room that is moving from downtown skyscrapers right into the home. Working at home either on household accounts or work brought home from the office requires a well-organized, comfortable work area. You can have that office—file drawers and all—even in close quarters. Your office might be a desk and bookshelf arrangement placed in your entry-way or on a wide upstairs landing. If you're lucky enough to have a guest room, why not use it as an office? A fresh scheme of green, yellow and white would provide pleasant work surrounding and a warm welcome for guests as well. Many people let their dining alcove double as a home office, using the dining table as a desk.

OFF-WHITE

A warm color—white with a touch of yellow pigment. Off-white rooms can be very effective, and the most effective ones are those with furnishings of mellow tones and soft, happy paintings on the walls. Here's an off-white look that may appeal to you: Cover walls with off-white moire fabric, and hang off-white moire draperies at the windows, tied back with ivory cords. Cover living-room sofa and club chairs with an oyster-on-white damask. On fruitwood tables, place oriental jar lamps with off-white pleated shades. A white marble-top coffee table on a gilt base would be my choice for the occasional table in front of sofa. Carpet room in off-white and hang soft art on walls.

Office

OPAQUE

Lightproof—a necessity for window shades and lampshades. Opaque window shades are for people who like to sleep in the morning. I rarely if ever use a translucent window shade in a bedroom. And I do like opaque lampshades that give off light only through the top and bottom, in an intermittent pattern.

If a room is painted dark green, I sometimes paint the outsides of the lampshades dark green, too. The inside surfaces are generally a gold paper, to project a warm light. I very often use white opaque shades on chandelier candles—and many, many brass Georgian-style fixtures have I outfitted with black opaque paper shades.

ORGANIZED CLUTTER

A way of arranging everyday objects so they enhance your decor. Every home has clutter, books, hobbies and magazines; that's part of what life is about. My idea is to arrange and organize that clutter so it enhances your room.

Is your eyeglass case always lying out on a table? Why can't that eyeglass case be as attractive as any other accessory in your room? Choose a needlepoint case in cheery colors, or a tooled leather case in your favorite color. Magazines are fun to read but awful to look at when they're scattered around a room. Instead, arrange three or four on your coffee table, selecting those with the most colorful covers. Stow the rest in a large wicker basket, acrylic rack or colorful straw basket on the floor. Cigarette packs are clutter, but a cigarette box in wood, fabric, tortoise, straw or silver is attractive clutter. A kitchen collection of boxes, bottles and such is clutter, but a set of inexpensive glass cookie jars to hold food staples is attractive clutter.

ORIENTAL LOOK

The serene look of Japan, China and Korea—the look of lacquer work, shoji screens and tatami mats, of ginger jars and rattan. Orientals have known for centuries that a room needn't be crowded with furniture to be beautiful. In Japan, a room may contain nothing more than a few low tables and mats for seating, but it is beautiful indeed. Because of their simplicity, oriental furniture and accessories blend beautifully with the Western look of things. Chinese-style ginger-jar lamps have graced European-style end tables and have always looked right at home. And these days you often see Japanese shoji screens living happily in contemporary and traditional rooms. How pretty a shiny spot of red or black Chinese or Japanese lacquer work can look with today's natural look, with beiges, whites and warm browns. Try a red lacquered tray table in front of a beige sofa, or a black lacquered desk painted with pretty oriental motifs or a Chinese red lacquered credenza against beige walls and see that room come to life.

Oriental look

105

ORIENTAL RUGS

They dress up any floor. Everyone can use and enjoy beautiful oriental rugs. The antique rugs are considered by experts to be the more beautiful, but I personally have nothing against a good-quality new oriental, particularly for heavy traffic areas of the home.

Antique orientals in poor condition should not be passed up. You can use them for pillow covers for the sofa or floor. Look for ripped or badly worn rugs in antique shops. You can sew kilims—oriental rugs without pile—at home, using the heaviest sewing-machine needle and heaviest thread you can find. Pile rugs are best done on a heavy-duty machine by your local tailor or dressmaker.

If you're a traditionalist who wants to keep the rug on the floor, don't be scared off by the pattern of oriental rugs. The patterns are usually subtle enough to mix well with prints and patterned weaves used for upholstery, draperies and accessories.

OTTOMAN

A decorating "extra" that is always welcome. The traditional skirted ottomans with soft cushiony tops are still with us and always will be, I hope. But now there are plastic ottomans molded into delightful curves and covered with soft stretchy fabrics as well as Parsons-style ottomans with upholstered legs and cube ottomans topped with fat pillows.

It's easy to make your own ottoman, using a plywood cube or even a sturdy wood crate as a base. Simply tack layers of thick padding over the cube's top and sides and cover neatly with fabric, using nailheads, tape or braid to trim the edges. For extra softness, top with a fat upholstered cushion.

Today we use an ottoman for conversation grouping the way we once used an occasional chair. The ottoman will accommodate an extra guest at a party and can be used as a foot rest with a matching armchair.

Ottomans are also moving under tables,

Ottomans

106

where they are kept until extra seating is needed. You can keep two upholstered ottomans under the console table behind your sofa or under the entryway console table. Upholster the ottomans to match your living-room upholstery or have them covered in matching vinyl. In a zippy red, white and black contemporary room, the table and ottomans could be covered in black patent vinyl and finished with glittery silver nailheads.

In a traditional room, you could use tobacco brown leather or leather-look vinyl and brass nailheads.

A hassock is an ottomon that is completely upholstered and is best when it has roller casters so it can easily be pulled up for conversation groupings. I often use a pair of hassocks as coffee-table pull-ups. As they are upholstered to the base, the casters are recessed and not seen.

Oval-back chair

OVAL-BACK CHAIRS

Chairs of the Louis XVI period that I often use in dining rooms and as living-room pull-up pieces.

Oval-back chairs help create a dining room as graceful as the following. Walls are covered with a Chinoiserie wallcovering, and the floor is richly stained marquetry. The dining table is glass, and the chandelier is a Marie-Thérèse with some amethyst prisms. The chairs are oval-back French armchairs, upholstered in a soft stripe—maybe a combination of melon, pale green, beige and soft rose.

OVERDONE

The worst decorating look! Know where to stop. Every window in the house doesn't have to be undercurtained, overdraped, swagged and fringed. Every wall doesn't have to be flocked and heavily laden with pictures and prints and objets d'art. Every floor in the house doesn't have to be carpeted and then

area-rugged. Every tabletop doesn't have to be accessorized with trinkets. Keep your decorating look easy!

OVERSTUFFED

The generous look for upholstered furniture. It's look I love. Plump, cushy upholstered furniture is definitely with us. And I say hurrah—I'll take a soft, plump sofa or chair any day. If you're in the market for a sofa, please consider buying an overstuffed Lawson or Tuxedo-style sofa with cushions filled with down or a soft synthetic material. Cover your couch in a tiny paisley print if your look is country French; with a nubby beige wool or cotton if you like the natural look; with velvet for a rich elegant setting. It may cost more than you had planned to spend, but the extra expense is well worth it because a classic sofa with heavenly soft cushions goes with any decor.

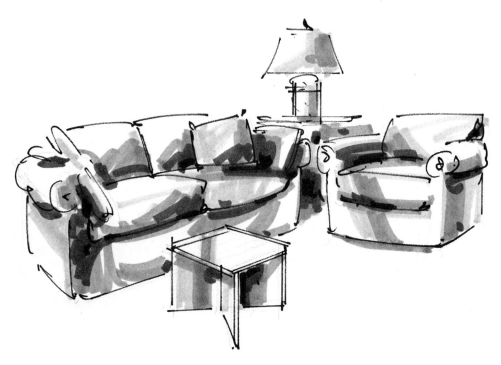

Overstuffed furniture

The overstuffed look is in pillow furniture, too. Pillow furniture, which started with young people tossing huge, colorful pillows on the floor for seating, has grown up. You can now buy modular pillow furniture that snaps together, as well as plump pillow furniture raised off the floor on wood frames.

P

PAINT

The most fabulous decorating tool. Don't judge it by the liquid color in the can. Always paint a small section of a wall, let it dry, and judge the color before covering all wall surfaces. Dark liquid paint colors tend to turn lighter; light liquid paint colors turn darker.

Use lacquer on your walls only if the surface is completely smooth. Any high-gloss color on walls will show every plaster imperfection. If walls are in poor condition, use only flat paint.

PAIRS

The basis of the "two of everything" matching look, which I do not favor. I have never advocated decorating with pairs. I do not think that a sofa must be flanked by a pair of matching end tables. If you do have matching tables, there is no rule that says the lamps on the tables must match; try a ginger jar on one table and a glass column lamp on the other. I do not think a living room has to house a pair of matching club chairs. One lounge chair teamed with a wing chair could look

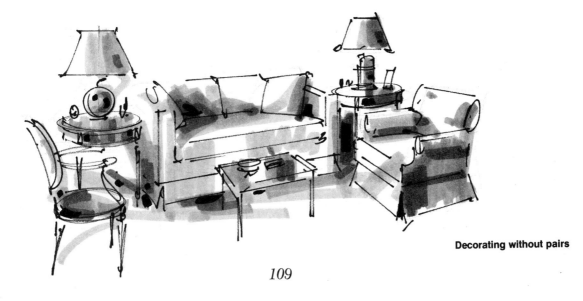

Decorating without pairs

109

very nice. If you do have matching club chairs, don't buy matching end tables, matching occasional chairs, matching pillows for the sofa, a pair of matching pictures to hang over your sofa and a pair of matching wall sconces for the right and left of your breakfront. Pairs should be used in a restrained way.

I might add that there are certain situations that demand the paired look. I do think a twin-bedded room needs matching headboards. A guest room would look mighty strange with one headboard of brass and the other of cane or rattan.

PANELING

The warm look of wood for walls. There are many ways to achieve the wood-paneled look without much money—and without wood. There are vinyl wallcoverings in wood grains and hardboard panels in wood tones. And there's *faux bois* painting—a way of painting walls, beams, doors to imitate the look of fine wood.

For walls that are badly cracked and pitted, use wood paneling. To break up the wall of a high-ceilinged room, wood panel up to the chair rail, with paint or paper for the upper half. Most people use wood paneling with the family room and the den, but I also like to see it in other rooms—as, for instance, in an attractive kitchen featuring walls "paneled" in a light pecan vinyl. Wood trim, cabinet doors and window shutters are painted tomato red. The floor is decorated with a bright Spanish tile design of pecan brown, tomato red and sunny yellow on a white background. Cookware and accent pieces are sunny yellow and tomato red. Green plants in interior window boxes, painted red, complete the cheery decor.

Pecky cypress is a very popular soft wood, with many deep irregular channels. In its natural color it gives a country look when used for walls in the family room. At windows, the

Pecky cypress

boards should be treated with a sealer. I'd use matching louver shutters with natural stain and flooring of rich country emerald green. Sofa and chair upholstery would be a country garden multicolored floral or a vivid plaid.

I also like white-painted pecky cypress for walls, especially with white rattan furnishings.

PAPER-BAG BROWN

A decorating color borrowed from the lowly brown bag.

To me, its beauty is in its neutrality—it goes well with any color you can name. It's an excellent wallcover, but don't limit yourself to walls. I like it for upholstery and accessories, too.

Paper-bag brown makes a rugged look for a boy's room, a den or a bachelor's bathroom. It's a rustic look for country kitchens and living rooms. And it can also be elegant-looking—try it in a traditional French living room to give a fresh, natural look that's so popular today.

Start by painting walls paper-bag brown and all trim and ceiling white. Paint the frames of your bergère chairs and your sofa a fresh white. Upholster the chairs in paper-bag brown velvet. For the sofa, choose a rich chocolate-brown velvet, with toss pillows of raspberry pink and buttercup yellow. At the windows hang raspberry-pink cotton moire draperies over white matchstick roller blinds. Carpet the room in pale jade green. For end tables against those warm brown walls, go white—Parsons tables, cubes or painted wood. End-table lamps can be buttercup-yellow jar lamps with white shades.

PARSONS TABLE

A modern table design named for the Parsons School of Design in New York City, where it originated. The Parsons table looks at

Parsons tables

PATCHWORK

A textile design that has moved from the Early American bedroom into every room of the house. Patchwork is no longer for quilts only. You can now find patchwork lamp bases, dishes, wallcoverings, tablecloths, yard goods and sheets. And why not? Patchwork with its many colors and designs is so easy to decorate with.

Multicolor patchwork vinyl on walls can accommodate any number of color schemes—it even allows you to change your color schemes with the seasons. If your bedroom patchwork wallcovering is blue and apricot on a white ground, you can use warm melon for bedspread and curtains in winter and pale ice blue in summer. If your room needs a dramatic focal point, patchwork comes to the rescue. You can hang a real patchwork quilt on the wall. You can upholster a sofa with patchwork. And you can cut up an old quilt or two to make a bevy of toss pillows for a blah sofa.

home in almost any kind of interior you can name, from elegant French period rooms to rustic country settings. And happily, they come in finishes and looks as varied as can be: leather-covered, gilded, lacquered—you can even buy them unfinished to decorate yourself with paint, fabric, decoupage, stencils or wood stains.

Decorating a Parsons table is a breeze, thanks to its squared-off shape and straight legs. Try decoupage on a pair of Parsons end tables for an Early American living room. Cut out pictures of eagles, ships, flowers or any design you favor. Glue the pictures, overlapping them, to an unfinished Parsons table and coat with layers and layers of a clear varnish. Topped with lamps made of tea cannisters, copper or even simple ginger jars, those tables will be conversation pieces.

Patchwork wall hanging

PATIO DOORS

A decorating problem with many attractive solutions. Why do people feel they must swathe those glass doors in yards and yards of heavy drapery fabric when the whole purpose of patio doors is to let in lots and lots of light? When privacy is no problem, I frequently treat patio doors with nothing more than a great display of plants hanging from the ceiling or standing on the floor. To frame a patio door attractively without overwhelming it, I may suggest a plywood frame covered in fabric or filled with summery white lattice.

If you live in the South, or if your door gets too much sun, cut the glare with narrow-slat venetian or matchstick blinds. Two or three panels hung floor to ceiling is a practical treatment, since it allows you to control the panels separately for easy access to the doors. When draperies or curtains are a must, I favor lightweight cotton looped casually, café-style, from a fat pole. The curtain panel covering the door could also be hung from a narrow rod hinged to the wall so that it swings away when the door is in use.

If you're stumped by the narrow wall space that often flanks the patio door, try built-to-fit wooden bookcases. If there's room above the door, continue the shelf treatment right up and over the door. It's a great place for displaying collectibles and an attractive way to treat the patio door without resorting to the heavy look of draperies.

PATTERN-ON-PATTERN

One of my favorite decorating looks, the pattern-on-pattern look goes way back in history. The Orientals and the Arabs have always known how to mix patterns. And what about our great-grandmothers, who mixed patterns daringly in their lovely patchwork quilt designs?

The most important rule is that the patterns must have some relationship to one another in color, scale and mood. Another rule is that stripes and geometrics are the easiest patterns to work with, along with florals or abstracts with some colors.

If you want to try your hand at mixing patterns, here's a bedroom scheme for you: Walls are papered in a cool variegated stripe of leaf green and white. The floral bedspread and floor-length draperies feature the same green foliage complementing blossoms of peach, coral, lemon yellow and cornflower blue, all on a white background.

For carpeting, I picture a tiny all-over geometric in the same green and white as the wallcovering. Bedside tables are white. And for lamps, use a small-scale floral in the bedspread colors. Pleated lampshades are white.

Remember, with flowered prints, to mix as you would a flower garden. Use full-scale flowers on trellis for background wallcovering and for draperies. Cover accent pieces, such as chairs and pillows, with small flower prints.

Patio doors

Pattern-on-pattern

Pedestals

PEDESTAL

A column sometimes round, sometimes octagonal, sometimes hexagonal, sometimes square—used as a plant or sculpture stand, or to display something you like.

Pedestals come in all shapes and sizes and in every kind of material. I have used them in glass for sculptures and in chrome-and-glass for plant stands.

Place a group of low pedestals together for a coffee table. Use one as a plant stand in your dining-room window or use a pair of them to display large urns. Use a modern pair as sofa end tables in the living room with modern lamps for an effective look.

PERENNIALS

My word for decorating classics that grow more beautiful with the passing years. I can

name three perennials guaranteed to stand you in good stead for years: the sturdy Parsons table; a classic, well-constructed Lawson or Tuxedo-style sofa; and ginger-jar lamps.

PEWTER

An all-American favorite found today in the form of flatware, tableware and decorative accessories such as lamps. I love those gleaming pewter accessories, but what about that rich silvery pewter color for walls, upholstery and carpets?

Try this colonial-inspired pewter-gray dining-room scheme and you'll see what I mean. Paint the walls in rich pewter, with ceilings, doors and moldings painted a fresh white. Paint the floor white, too, and protect it with layers of non-yellowing Polyurethane.

For dining, use a practical, pretty Parsons-type table of daffodil-yellow laminate. Team that modern table with high-backed,

pine ladder-back chairs with rush seats. Seat pads can be an Americana patchwork design of lemon yellow, pewter, burnt orange and white. And use that same patchwork to line a pine or maple hutch in which you display pewter mugs, pewter bread-and-butter plates and pewter candlesticks.

At windows, hang white bamboo roller blinds under simple swag valances of the patchwork print, and light up your cozy pewter dining room with a colonial-style chandelier of pewter.

PHOTOGRAPHS

An inexpensive and attractive way to decorate. Framed photographs of family and friends can look charming covering the entire wall of a family room or den. Another imaginative way is to have them blown up to poster size. Two or three ancestral portraits in giant format in your entryway will make a

Decorating with photographs

dramatic and personal statement that will charm your guests. Or thrill a child with a life-size poster of himself on his door.

I love the look of framed photographs on end tables, particularly when the frames are pretty. And they needn't cost a lot. You can buy five-and-dime frames and cover them with fabric or ribbon. You can also paint or de-coupage them, or gild them with real gold leaf. And, yes, it's okay to hang family pictures and portraits over the living-room sofa. I have never relegated the people I love—or their pictures—to the back hall.

PIANO

The most decorative musical instrument. Pianos play a happy decorating tune—one you can play anywhere in the house as long as you keep the piano away from radiators and windows (experts tell me extremes of temperature and humidity are bad for the piano). Don't

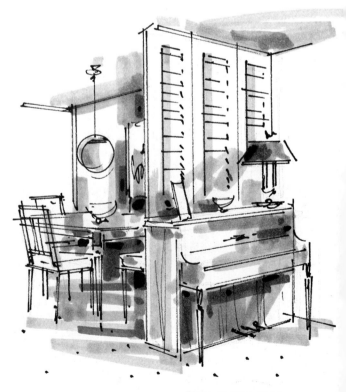

Piano as room divider

relegate it to the living room. It's perfectly proper for a child to have a piano in his own room to practice on; it needn't be a fine instrument either—an old spinet would be fine. And if the finish is not in good repair, why not paint that spinet a happy color?

A spinet piano can also be used as a room divider provided it is placed at a right angle to a wall. One studio-apartment dweller I know used a walnut spinet to divide the living area from the dining area in her home. A louver shutter was installed from the top of the piano to the ceiling to close off the two areas completely, and the shutters were stained to match the piano's finish.

And a word to those who use their grand piano top as an extra table: I'm all for it, if discretion is used. No vases filled with water, please. And remember, a shawl over the top of your piano will protect the finish and will also muffle the tone to a certain extent. Use a pretty old paisley shawl or a fringed, embroidered shawl.

PICTURES

Hung correctly, in the right frames, pictures can add more to a room than any other accessory. Here are some pointers that I want to share with you. First, whatever you do, don't hang pictures on every available wall surface, unless you are after a picture-store effect. I think they should be hung only on surfaces that seem empty without them.

When hanging a picture grouping over a sofa, a buffet, a console or small pier table, never let the grouping be wider than the piece of furniture under it. I think pictures hung close together give a unified look to a wall. So, if you have a grouping of bird prints of different sizes and shapes, put them over the hunt table in the family room and hang them close together—not frame against frame, however. Leave some wall space in between. And I hang them geometrically so the frames form a square or rectangle. If you have four pictures

of the same size, all framed alike, my choice would be to hang them in a square over the sofa, for instance, or in a straight line over a long table, or vertically above each other over a small step table. If you must hang pictures stepwise, do so only on a staircase. Otherwise, I like to see a continuous straight line formed by the bottoms of those frames.

To hang groups of pictures of various sizes, subjects and shapes, try framing and matting everything alike. I once saw sixteen prints all in simple gold frames and matted in forest green—how great they looked against a red felt wall. For pictures of the same size, you can add punch by matting each in a different color.

Picture grouping

PIE-CRUST TABLE

An eighteenth-century English table that is a decorating classic. This scalloped-edge classic is found in the most beautiful homes in the world. It is good as a sofa end table or between a pair of chairs. It could be used in a dining-room bay as the spot to display a silver coffee service. A pie-crust table can go anywhere in the home.

Pie crust table

PILLOWS

The "soft touch" no room should be without—colorful pillows to brighten a drab room, ruffled pillows to soften a too-tailored room, pillows to add soft comfort to hard chairs, and pillows on a grand scale to supplement conventional furniture or substitute for it entirely.

PINK

A color you can use everywhere in the house. Pink can pack a lot of punch and shouldn't be reserved for the bedroom and the bath. Use it in the living room, the dining room, the family room.

Navy blue and pink is a sophisticated combination for the L-shaped living room/ dining room that's so popular these days. Paint walls white, and carpet in dark navy blue. Upholster your sofa in a floral print of navy, white and pink. For club chairs, I'd like to see a lattice print of pink and white. At windows,

hang draperies and a valance of your floral sofa print, and line your valance in solid powder pink. To tie your dining area into the pink-and-navy scheme, use the solid-pink fabric to cover the dining-chair seats, and welt them in navy blue. Above your dining-room sideboard, hang a mirror with a wide frame covered in your navy-and-pink print. For spice, I would use tomato-red accents throughout.

Green and pink are another happy color team. For a different look in a Florida-style room, start with a grass-green shag carpet underfoot. Cover walls in a jungle print of pinks, greens and canary yellow. Paint wicker furniture the palest pink you can find, and slipcover in green-and-white gingham checks. At your windows, hang pale-pink matchstick blinds.

PLAID

A lively geometric design originally found in Scottish tartans. I love plaid. Plaid today is a

Plaid in a bedroom

perennial pattern with many different looks—from the oriental Siamese to rustic Americana. If you favor the natural look, use a plaid of natural beiges and browns upholstery against walls of matching plaid. On natural-wood floors, a Navajo rug of tans, grays and browns would team beautifully with the plaid. For a pretty look for frilly bedrooms or bathrooms, there are many pretty plaids in soft pastel tints to enhance the femininity of any room. And they blend so well with that other pretty perennial, the floral print. To see what I mean, picture a little girl's room with pink and white plaid walls and bedspread and draperies in a floral print of petal pink, lemon yellow, sky blue, apricot and grass green on a white ground.

PLANTS

Nothing adds life like plants. Just be sure your plants are suited to your scheme: no cacti in frilly bedrooms. But have all the cacti you want in a rugged redwood-furnished family room. Create a jungle environment for a basement playroom with lots of large tree-like plants—rubber plants, Ficus Benjamina trees, palms in natural clay pots—and light them artificially. Lay a floor of black and white zebra-print vinyl; cover the sofa in a rough-textured burnt-orange cotton and choose cotton sling chairs of chocolate brown.

Turn a sunny bedroom into a Victorian solarium with live ferns, pink geraniums, begonias and palms. Hang the flowering plants in white wicker baskets in front of the sunny windows. Ferns and palms can go on the floor in gleaming white porcelain planters. Have a four-poster bed of chalk white with pale green-and-white gingham blanket covers and pillow shams. A natural-finish light wood armoire would be the perfect storage piece. And for relaxing among the plants, I would select a chaise longue upholstered in deep rose.

PLASTIC

A dirty word to some, but not to the forward-looking decorator. I do not like certain uses of plastic in decorating—plastic slipcovers and lampshade covers, for instance. But there's a positive side to the plastics story. There is plastic furniture in cheery colors and gleaming finishes. There's plastic for walls in textures and prints of every description. There's even attractive plastic fabric for upholstery—vinyl suedes and leathers are two handsome examples. These days it's possible to decorate an entire room in plastic, and that

room will be attractive, easy to care for and inexpensive. Plastic items are perfect for children's rooms, retirement apartments, family rooms, dining areas and any room where easy care is a requirement.

Try the plastic way of decorating in your family room. Cover walls in tortoise-shell vinyl. Upholster a sofa and chairs in a coin-gold vinyl suede, and go gold for wall-to-wall shag carpeting, too. Cover a bergère chair in lipstick-red patent vinyl. And how about placing a handsome chocolate-brown molded-plastic game table and chairs in a corner of your family room? What a perfect place for games and for serving light suppers and snacks!

PORCH

An outdoor area that's having an impact on interior decoration. I like the outdoorsy look of a porch so much, I'm in favor of using it for indoor decor, too. Why not use white wicker in a sky-blue bedroom with a pretty

Plastic furniture

floral fabric accompaniment in sunshine yellow, peach, peony pink and greens? Why not an awning stripe for family-room upholstery? Why not lacy wrought iron and trellis for a summery entryway done up in sharp greens and sunny yellows?

Or how about an outdoorsy porch scheme in the tropical mood built around bamboo-look sofa and chairs of parrot green and white molded plastic? Chairs can be upholstered in a carefree floral print of orange peel, lemon, lime and white. Add a glass-topped table or two and a skirted table covered in a pretty stripe of lemon and white. For walls, tropical stucco painted fresh lemon yellow would be nice. Floors can be white vinyl planking, and at windows repeat those lemon stripes in laminated window shades trimmed in parrot green.

Decorating with a poster

POSTERS

An inexpensive and colorful way to decorate walls, and not only in informal rooms. To my way of thinking, big, bright posters can make a decorating splash anywhere in the house. Inexpensive posters are great for children's rooms just because they're inexpensive and can be replaced as the child grows and changes. I like to see them used here in headboard fashion.

Many museums, both here and abroad, print posters to advertise showings of paintings and scupltures. One I admired recently was a reproduction, in warm russets, greens and golds, of a painting by an old Dutch master. In a narrow gold frame, behind glass, hung on a forest-green wall, that poster would be very much at home in a formal period setting.

Because of their size, posters give you a lot of color and design for a relatively small amount of money. Another elegant way of showing them is on an easel. There are beautiful easels in bamboo, brass and wood that make handsome stands for large, framed posters. Put one in the corner of your living room and shine a ceiling spotlight on it to turn a drab nook into a mini-gallery.

In the past, framing a poster was often the most expensive part of it. Today you can have them laminated inexpensively. The poster is mounted on a stiff backing, and decorative tape is then applied around the edge to provide a narrow "frame." Finally the backed poster is laminated with a clear plastic film.

PRIMARY COLORS

Red, yellow and blue. You can decorate a room in the primary colors if you are careful. For a lively dining room, paint the walls royal blue, the ceiling red and all trim white. Cover dining-room floor with red and white tiles laid on the diagonal. The curtains can be a red, white, blue and yellow geometric print. Use the same print on white framed dining-room chairs around a white Parsons table.

PRIZED POSESSION

A good starting point for a winning room scheme. When you're stuck for decorating inspiration, use a favorite object as the starting point. Your inspiration may come from a colorful heirloom quilt or from a shell collection, a vase or a special lamp. Or you may have a collection of Wedgwood that would be a great inspiration for a restful dining-room scheme.

Walls could be that soft Wedgwood blue in a matte finish with the trim painted frosty white to imitate the famous white frosting used on Wedgwood china.

On a dark-stained wood floor, lay a chinese-style patterned area rug of Wedgwood, powder blue and cream.

For dining chairs and table, I would choose rich walnut with seat pads in a stripe of Wedgwood, cream and soft, soft pink with just a pencil-thin line of old gold. Use the stripe at windows for elegant swag and jabot draperies hung over white sheers.

The focal point of the room—your Wedgwood collection—can be displayed in a gleaming wood corner cabinet. And to illuminate the scene, a crystal chandelier, fitted with tiny white tucked shades, would be my choice.

PROVINCIAL

The pretty, colorful look of the French countryside—blue skies, herb-covered hillsides, charming shuttered villas and, of course, French Provincial furniture and fabrics. Always keep the look light and sunny—no heavy draperies. No velvet or brocades. No gilding. For your French Provincial furniture, use that great contribution to decorating: the Provincial print. In fabric or wallcovering it can be flowered, striped or geometric. It is always

Provincial look

122

small in scale, regular in pattern and gay in appearance. And Provincial prints offer a plus—they are easy to mix with other prints. Try a Provincial paisley with a ticking stripe, for instance. Or a Provincial floral with a windowpane check.

PUMPKIN

A color for year-round decorating. Pumpkin is one of my favorite decorating colors. I would like a living room with pumpkin-colored walls and white door trim, golden-yellow carpet and draperies of white moire, trimmed in pumpkin and gold. Pumpkin velvet would be soft and inviting on the cushy living-room sofa, and I'd cover club chairs in a pumpkin damask on white silk. I'd accent the end tables with shiny brass lamps (white lamp shades, please), and for punch I'd accessorize the glass-top table with some brass pieces—an ashtray and cigarette lighter—and for fun, a red-lacquered melon-shaped box, too!

Pumpkin goes with just about every other color. A den I saw recently in California had wood walls, pumpkin-colored carpeting and linen draperies of a pumpkin, apple-green, chocolate-brown and azure-blue block design. The block design was used on a club chair and ottoman in the room, and it was used as the cover for throw pillows on the chocolate-brown leather Chesterfield sofa.

Think pumpkin and yellow flowers entwined with green leaves on a white ground as the fanciful floral print wallcovering in your kitchen. How smashing the design would look in a kitchen that had a green vinyl floor, white cabinets, white fixtures and countertops of yellow.

Think pumpkin when you want to give some dash to a gray-tiled bathroom. Paint the walls with a pumpkin semi-gloss enamel, and install a gray-painted louver shutter at the window. Shower curtain can be a gray-on-white geometric print with a wide pumpkin border. Accessories in the bathroom might be white wicker shelves filled with white and chromium perfume and cotton jars. Bath towels can be black, white, gray and pumpkin. And for a bathroom carpet on the gray tile floor, choose pumpkin!

PURPLE

A color I like with lots of pink, apple green, sky blue and white. For your living room, why not plum-purple walls and white trim? Your sofa can be covered in pale cosmos pink, and your club chairs can be upholstered in a soft flowered print of purples, pinks, apple greens and sky blues on a white background. Window draperies and valances can be the flower print, too, lined in soft pink. On occasional chairs, I suggest a sky-blue and apple-green stripe print. When making lampshades for big white jar-style lamps, choose a blush-pink silk.

123

Q

QUARRY TILE

Clay floor tiles in nature's own colors. Many people have quarry tile floors in the entryway or the kitchen, but why relegate quarry tile to those areas of the house? I love quarry tile anywhere there's a floor. And its popularity is spreading simply because it's durable, versatile, natural and easy to care for. Just simple mopping keeps it looking super.

In an Early American living room I picture terra-cotta quarry tile with beige linen-covered walls. At windows, I see draperies of black, beige and chocolate-brown plaid. And topping that terra-cotta tiled floor, how about a braided rug in the same natural colors? Sofa upholstery can be emerald-green corduroy, accented with toss pillows of beige, chocolate, black and white. And I would upholster a pair of wood-framed easy chairs in the drapery plaid.

QUARTZ

The most popular quartz is rock crystal. Many is the lamp base of rock crystal I have used in my decoration. Rock-crystal paper-

Quarry tile floor

125

weights are collectibles, and in my own living room there is a rock-crystal natural sculpture. There are many other colors of quartz. Rose quartz is the second most popular, and you'll also find hexagonal crystals of amethyst, topaz, yellow, red and brown.

QUEEN ANNE

An important era in furniture history. During the Queen Anne period, from 1702 to 1714, the graceful curved line became important. Chair backs curved and chair legs curved into Chinese-inspired claw-and-ball feet. Oriental lacquer work was all the rage, and tea drinking and tea tables of all kinds—tilt-top, pie-crust top and gallery top—spread across England. And everyone was busy collecting things oriental—china in particular and china cabinets in which to display those collections.

You can still find many fine reproductions of Queen Anne-style furniture today. Those classic Queen Anne styles have never really gone out of fashion. But be warned: The Queen Anne look is a rich look, best used as a decorative accent. In a living room decorated the natural way in beige or gray tones or in pretty pastels, add dramatic punch with a black lacquered Queen Anne-style china cabinet or desk. For softness and flair in a contemporary dining room, team your glass-and-steel table or your Parsons-style table with a set of Chinese-red Queen Anne chairs. I picture those chairs grouped around a fir-tree-green Parsons table against walls papered in a plaid of sand beige, Chinese red and fir-tree green above a sand-beige-painted dado.

QUILTING

The soft, puffy look of padded, stitched fabric. Who says quilts and the quilted look must be relegated to beds? I like the quilted look for upholstery, and I enjoy it on walls and ceilings, too. Quilting adds an extra dimension of luxury and eye appeal to any room in the

Queen Anne Style

house. How about a quilted silver-foil wallcovering for bathroom walls? Or a quilted satin headboard in the bedroom? Or quilted upholstery in the living room? Almost any fabric can be quilted, you know—cottons, satins, velvets, even suede and leather.

A family room I'm designing will have the quilted look all the way. Walls are to be covered in chocolate-brown suede cloth—quilted, of course. Trim will be painted Chinese red, and the ceiling will be sheet-mirrored for airiness. There will be two buttery soft leather sofas in a warm tan. Club chairs will be upholstered in a quilted cotton geometric print of sharp green, chocolate brown, royal purple, Siamese pink and Chinese red on a black background. The carpet will be chocolate-brown shag. Draperies in the geometric print will hang under a quilted valance of the same fabric. I've selected contemporary brass and glass end tables, and their lamps will be brass cubes with white shades—and the brass lamp bases are quilted. Yes, metal can be quilted too!

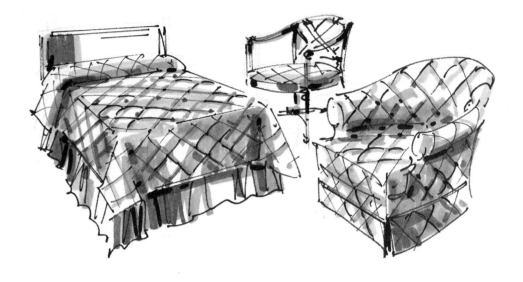

Quilted fabrics

R

RADIATOR

A modern necessity that is often a decorating problem. Concealing the ugly radiator is a challenge that almost everyone faces at some time or another. If your ugly radiator bulges out from under a window and gets in the way of draperies, try boxing in the radiator attractively and using bamboo shades, shutters or sill-length curtains. Make sure that the box has some kind of openwork in front, such as lattice, wicker, pierced wood or metal cane, so that the heat can escape.

If your under-the-window radiator is the flat type, sheer curtains can be used in front of it. Hang tie-back or loose drapery panels on either side. For the radiator window with no view I like to use a screen to conceal both radiator and window. Again, some type of openwork material should be used.

In informal rooms, such as kitchens, children's bedrooms or certain ultramodern rooms, I sometimes make no effort to conceal the radiator, especially if it's an old-fashioned type. In fact, I may paint that radiator a bright, peppy color just for fun. In a child's room, hang a washable, flowered geometric

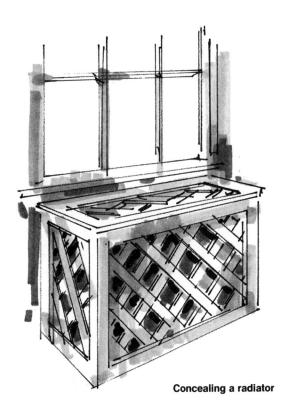

Concealing a radiator

wallcovering of primary blue, red and yellow. Paint radiator, window frames and doors fire-engine red. At windows, hang red-framed shutters, lined with primary-blue cotton. The carpet can be red. And for fitted bedspread, use canary yellow, welted in blue.

RAGS

Turn them into decorating riches. Rags are not for dusting only. Clean, attractive scraps cut from scarcely worn clothing or left over from home-sewing projects can be turned into boudoir pillows edged with lace or eyelet. People are creating thick braided rugs from woolen scraps or turning cotton scraps into patchwork creations of all kinds from quilts to curtains to table skirts.

You could decorate a little girl's room the rag way with crazy-patch curtains, a braided rug and patchwork quilt on the bed. Use cotton prints in clear pastels for the patchwork and pastel woolen scraps for the rug. The patchwork can be done "crazy-style," meaning that square patches can be joined at random, and the work can be done on the machine.

RECLINER

America's favorite chair. Recliners are becoming beautiful as well as comfortable. There are low-backed Lawson-style recliners and there are delicately proportioned ones suitable for the bedroom. I have even seen handsome leather-covered wing-style recliners that would be at home in an elegant nineteenth-century London club or in a comfortable modern den. And the best news is that recliners are now made so that they don't need tilt-back space. This makes them ideal for small rooms where furniture must go against the wall.

RED

The most exciting of all colors. There is not a color that doesn't work with red. A red, Christmas-green, sky-blue and pale-yellow room is a happy one. A red, chocolate-brown and beige scheme is popular with young bachelors. A red, purple and bittersweet orange scheme is for those who like the contemporary scene. A red, pink and white scheme and a red, white and black one have been popular for ages.

Here's a red scheme I like for the kitchen. Paint the ceiling sky blue and install bright-red vinyl tiles on the floor. Use white cabinets with bright-red laminate interior surfaces. The counter tops and splash-backs can be bright-red laminate also. Cover kitchen walls with strawberry designed wall vinyl, and decorate the kitchen windows with bright-red louver shutters. White kitchen chairs can have kelly-green seat pads.

Recliner

REFECTORY TABLE

A long, heavy rectangular table often of Renaissance design. There was a time when people were throwing away refectory tables in favor of lighter, more modern styles. Happily, people have learned that a refectory table can be used in a modern interior. I love the look of an ornate refectory table lacquered white and placed behind a sofa in a contemporary blue-and-white room. And I would like to see a bleached oak refectory table in an entryway with shiny black patent vinyl walls, bleached woodwork and beige sisal matting on the floor.

You could use a dark oak refectory table in a cozy family room as a desk. Cover walls in a red tartan and lay an emerald-green shag carpet underfoot. Pair the table with a high-backed Jacobean chair lacquered bright red. Line one wall with bookcases of rich wood.

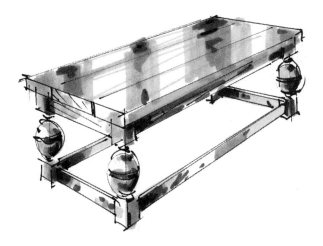

Refectory table

Regency style

REGENCY

That great style developed in England under George IV. I am definitely an English Regency person. I love this style with its fabulous designs greatly influenced by Chinese and Egyptian motifs. Regency furniture was often lacquered in the Chinese manner, and it was common to see black lacquered chests with gold trim. It was also common to see designs in mahogany, rosewood and satinwood furniture, and bamboo trimmings on crown moldings, doorways and furniture. If you have ever seen the beautiful Brighton Pavilion, you know what the Regency style is.

RENAISSANCE

A European furniture style dating from about 1400 to 1600. The Renaissance way of decorating was not a comfortable one by today's standards; furniture was squared off and seats were made of wood. But certain Renaissance styles—the refectory table and X-chair, for example—have lived on to the present and make impressive accent pieces in today's homes. For an authentic Renaissance at-

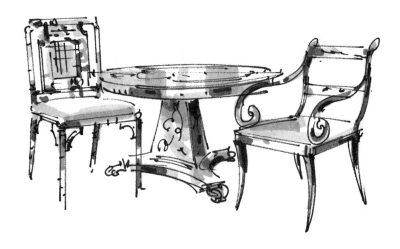

mosphere (and this applies to large rooms only), floors should be tiled in natural terracotta and walls should be white stucco. The look is even better if you have a cathedral ceiling. For more Renaissance flair, add a tall wrought-iron candelabra holding fat white candles.

RESORT LOOK

The look of tropical paradise places. Whether you live in the sunny South or in overcoat country, you can create a resort look in your own home with wallpaper, paint and furniture.

Lend a Caribbean air to your bathroom by papering walls in a tropical jungle print of green leaves on a white ground and painting the ceiling tropical sky blue. Or turn your breakfast nook into a tropical paradise by tacking white trellis strips to walls of hibiscus pink and covering seats of white chairs with a print of pink and chocolate-brown blooms on a white ground.

If new furniture is to be purchased, think wicker. Choose pieces with either the natural look or a light, bright lacquer finish.

Try the resort look in your bedroom against a backdrop of walls papered in a geranium print of reds, pinks and greens on a white ground. Upholster the headboard in a matching fabric and choose parrot-green wicker for night tables and an easy chair. Upholster the chair in a green-and-white plaid, and use curtains of the same plaid at windows. Dressers can be lacquered white and trimmed with parrot green.

RESTORATION

The name of today's decorating game. You can recreate the past in your home if you want to. I like the old mullion windows, the old plank doors, the old wood beam timbers, the really old antique brass bathroom fixtures.

And do not trade the old sofa for the new.

You are better off reconditioning and recovering a good, old, solid sofa frame than spending money on a new sofa with a frame that is not as good or as sturdy as the old. Yesterday's products were great, considering the durability of some modern ones.

ROCOCO

Louis XV's favorite decorating style. Louis XV was famous for his profusion of carved rococo rock-and-shell motifs around the cornices, mantlepieces and windows, over doors and on wainscots. He also used a lot of flowers, birds, fruits and branches in his wall decor. We don't design many rococo rooms today—there are no carvers about to do the work, and homeowners don't want to pay for the costly job.

For a piece of rococo in your home, choose an elaborate carved console table mirror. There are a number of rococo mirror frames on the market. I like vertically hung console mirrors, about three by four feet.

Rococo style

132

ROMAN SHADES

Tailored pleated shades usually made of heavy fabric. When a tailored look at windows is called for, I call for Roman shades. They work well in prints, particularly tailored geometrics, crisp plaids and stripes. And they look super in solid-color fabrics—canvas, natural linen and duck are good choices. If you use a solid color, add a contrasting tape trim about one inch in from each edge. I love the tailored look of Roman shades at unusually tall windows where long, full draperies would overwhelm the rest of the room. And I like them at windows where there's no surrounding wall space for draperies to go.

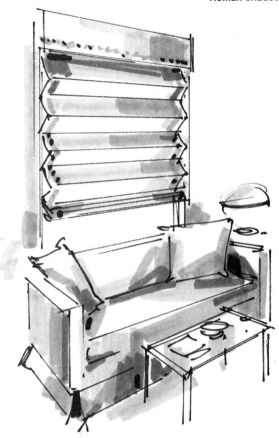

ROOM DIVIDER

A partition that separates one area of a room from another. I do not advocate spending money on built-in room dividers. They often cost more money to remove on moving day, and they rarely, if ever, fit into a new setup. A folding screen is my favorite room divider, and it can be used in many new ways in new places. Free-standing book shelves are good practical dividers. I find draperies on a track ridiculous as room dividers. I would rather see a partition made of beads.

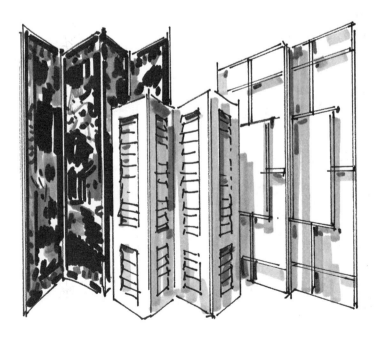

133

Ruffled curtains

RUFFLES

A soft, romantic look I love. If you love the country look of pine and maple furniture, bare floors and beams, ruffled chintz slipcovers are for you. Choose a soft floral print in misty mauve, petal pink, apricot and sky blue with green foliage on a white ground. And use ruffles at windows, too. I will never tire of white ruffled organdy curtains. I love them in country-style rooms, even when those rooms are in the city.

To give your bed the ruffled look, pile it high with ruffled pillows you make yourself. They can be edged with eyelet or with a fabric gathered into soft ruffles. For variety, make ruffles and pillow centers out of contrasting fabrics—pink-and-green floral for the ruffle, or make a striped center with a color-matched gingham border.

RUGS

An important accessory underfoot or on the wall. Whether your room is formal or casual, feminine or masculine, restful or busy, there's a rug for you. In a formal dining room

Rustic look

where delicate pastel colors and French furniture star, a sculptured Chinese-style area rug in subtle blues and cream would be a perfect touch. Daring modern rooms take well to the warmth of primitively colored rugs from Turkey, Mexico or India, either on the floor or, for something different, on the wall. I would like a light beige Rya rug in a living room with shiny chocolate-brown walls, ivory woodwork and curtains and textured beige upholstery. In a cozy bedroom wouldn't a fluffy white Greek flokati rug next to the bed be inviting?

I love the look of a rug against the polished wood of a parquet or wide-board floor, but rugs don't have to be laid over wood to look well. I like them over wall-to-wall carpeting, vinyl tile and sisal matting. You can even lay thin rugs on top of each other with the edges overlapping slightly.

RUSTIC

A decorating style inspired by peasant life. With today's taste for informal living, what could be more appropriate than decorating inspiration taken from rustic peasant life? Whether peasant styles of furniture, fabrics and accessories hail from Poland, Russia or Mexico, they all have certain similarities, such as bright, happy colors and charming floral motifs. Peasant-inspired floral fabrics with colorful borders are favorites of mine for children's rooms, kitchens and informal family rooms. If you would like just a tiny touch of the rustic look, try draping a floral printed challis scarf from eastern Europe over a skirted end table or breakfast table. Drapery inspiration can come from the rustic look, too, in the form of smocked drapery headings that look like the gathered necklines of peasant blouses.

S

SAND AND SEA

A decorating look inspired by carefree days at the seashore. The beach is a happy place to be and I would love to capture its mood in a room scheme to enjoy fifty-two weeks a year. Picture this fresh, breezy family-room scheme. Walls are painted sand beige, using textured sand paint, and the carpet is crunchy sand-beige sisal matting. The ceiling is fresh sky blue. For upholstery, I envision canvas in beach-umbrella stripes of sunshine yellow, sky blue and sand beige. And why not personalize that room with your own special collection of sea shells and driftwood? You can display it on open shelves with the natural look of sun-bleached wood. End tables can be sun-bleached wood, too. And for a coffee table, try a round glass top on a driftwood base.

SCALE

The all-important size relationship of one thing to another. If you have ever seen a large room where tiny pieces of furniture looked lost, you've seen an example of improper decorative scale. A large painting hanging over a tiny cigarette table is another example of improper scale. What is proper scale? While there's no rule of thumb, it's best to try to balance the size of a room with furniture and accessories of similar proportions—large, cushy sofas and chairs in large rooms; smaller, more delicate pieces in smaller rooms. Use tall pieces in tall rooms and short, squat ones in rooms with low ceilings. Fabric patterns should also be chosen accordingly, with large-scale patterns reserved for big rooms and small-scale designs used in diminutive rooms.

SCREENS

A great pick-me-up for a room with the architectural blahs. A screen or two can add drama, personality and softness to your home. Place a couple of brightly lacquered screens or screens papered to match walls in two corners of a boring room, and see it come to life. Or use two floor-to-ceiling mirrored screens near a window where they will reflect a park view outside and the room's exciting colors inside. In rooms with ugly views, I often use screens directly in front of windows.

Sand-and-sea look

Screens

138

If your living room looks more like a tunnel than a room, why not break it up with a screen? Place a three-panel screen partly across the room, and arrange your sofa and chair grouping on one side and your dining table and chairs on the other. If you're tired of the picture-grouping-above-the-sofa look, you can back your sofa with an interesting screen instead; it might be wallpapered, mirrored, painted or covered with fabric.

I recently used an inexpensive plywood screen to perk up a small, dark library. The owners wanted a cozy look, so I painted the walls a mood-setting hunter green. Bookcases on one wall were painted deep green, too. Underfoot was a wall-to-wall ribbed carpet of soft champagne beige accented with a colorful Moroccan rug of rich red, pumpkin and green. I upholstered two love seats in heavy beige basket-weave cotton and placed them at right angles to the wall opposite the bookcases. For color and excitement, I placed the plywood screen, lacquered Chinese red, against the wall. The love seats were piled high with toss cushions covered in a geometric print of pumpkin, Chinese red, hunter green and chocolate. Tie-back draperies of the same print were hung over Chinese-red louvered shutters.

Decorating with sea shells

SEA SHELLS

Decorating inspiration from nature. Never have I seen so many super shell looks in decorating. Fabric designers are coming up with shell-design fabrics galore, and accessory designers have gone wild with shell lamps, shell mirrors, shell-covered boxes and more.

Since shell colors are naturally harmonious, you can't go wrong with a shell-inspired scheme. Take the handsome conch shell with its dappled beige and white exterior and glowing pink interior. Wouldn't that color scheme translate beautifully into a dining room? I would paint walls soft conch-shell pink with white trim. At windows, hang beige and white

shell-print cotton draperies lined in soft conch-shell pink. Use the shell fabric for upholstery on a set of Parsons dining-room chairs grouped around a rectangular table lacquered sand beige. And when setting that table, I would use a basket of shells as a centerpiece and a group of shell candleholders fitted with white tapers. Set each place with pink linen place mats and matching napkins rolled in shell napkin rings.

SECONDARY COLORS

A color that is made by mixing any two of the three primary colors. Mix red with blue and you have purple; mix red with yellow and you have orange; mix blue with yellow and you have green. Let's plan a kitchen using these secondary colors. With white cabinets, use a checkerboard floor of green and white.

For countertops, go vivid orange plastic laminate. The wallcovering can be a floral print of orange, lavenders, purples and greens on a white background, and the kitchen curtains can be orange and white gingham check. Choose green enamel pots for kitchenware.

SEMAINIER

A tall chest with a drawer for every day of the week. (*Semaine* is French for *week*.) I think semainiers are very practical. The small drawers in the chest hold socks, underwear, jewelry, scarfs and handkerchiefs. When buying a reproduction of the piece be certain it has seven drawers. Some today come with only five or six drawers.

SHAKER

Furniture design known for its simple beauty. The Shakers were members of a religious sect started in the eighteenth century. They practiced great austerity in every aspect of life, and this carried over into their clean, simple furniture designs. Chairs are straight, yet comfortable. There is no carving or orna-

Shaker style

mentation, so Shaker pieces blend well with both contemporary and traditional decor.

Shaker decorating is ideal for those who live in cramped quarters. In a small dining room, for instance, I like a Shaker trestle table teamed with smart-looking low-backed Shaker chairs. The low backs let you push the chairs under the table when they're not in use! If the total austerity of the Shaker look is not your cup of tea, add some color and verve to your dining room with colorful rugs and cheerful paintings or posters in hot pink, reds, oranges and acid green against white walls.

SHAPE

Don't overlook the importance of shape in your decorating scheme. The most interesting rooms are those in which various shapes are played against one another. I have seen many rooms in which a long, narrow rectangular sofa was paired with two rectangular end tables, a rectangular coffee table and a pair of squared-off club chairs. They are almost as bad as rooms in which everything is unrelieved curves, from the semicircular sofa to the tub chairs to the circular area rug.

I always look for that special piece of furniture with the interesting shape: the semicircular hunt table, the circular tilt-top table, the fan-backed Windsor chair, the free-form molded foam seating units of ultra-contemporary design. One or two of these unusually shaped pieces is all you need to give a blah room new life.

If you have all the furniture you need but still would like to do some shaping up, there are many tricks to try. You can reshape a boxy room by installing a corner cupboard or some corner shelves, or by making an arrangement of tall plants in one corner. At windows, deep shaped valances covered in your drapery fabric add shape appeal. Shape up uninteresting walls by creating arches with stock molding; paint the moldings a contrasting color, or fill the "arches" with wallpaper murals.

SHAWLS

Decorative wearing apparel for the home. What with the resurgence of interest in handicrafts of late, what could be more timely than accessorizing rooms with the handmade beauty of shawls? I have seen giant-sized, handmade shawls used as bedspreads and even as throws on sofa beds. At a New England crafts fair not too long ago I purchased a gray-and-white alpaca and wool handwoven shawl with long, silky fringe that will be one accessory in an all-gray-and-white room I'm designing. If you're an antique-fancier, scout the shops for those jewel-tone wool paisley shawls that were made in Scotland years ago. They make great skirts for bedroom or living-room end tables, and they can become stunning toss-pillow covers.

If you've ever wondered how to dress up your dining table when it's not in use, consider draping it with a long scarf-type shawl. I favor the Mexican or South American ones in tangy shades of pumpkin, purple, wine, red and emerald green. Top the shawl with fat, colorful candles or a wicker basket full of green plants.

SHEETS

Bedcoverings, plus! These days sheets are being used on beds, on walls, as slipcovers, as curtains. And you don't have to settle for pale, washed-out florals or polite little candy stripes. Today we have batiks, Navajo designs, rich florals on dark or light backgrounds, Persian motifs and bold geometrics. And sheet patterns are now available in yard-goods form, so there's no time like the present to decorate with sheets.

Try doing a country-style dining room in sheets printed with rich pink and yellow roses, bluebells and green foliage on a white ground. Use the sheets shirred on the walls, and leave

Decorating with sheets

the woodwork natural. Ceiling and doors would be white. I picture a natural-wood floor topped with a needlepoint floral rug in shades of yellow, pink, green and blue on a cream ground. The table and chairs would be rustic bleached pine with seat pads of apple green, and the table would be set with rose-patterned quilted place mats, grass-green pottery and a centerpiece of pink and white geraniums with green leaves in a straw basket. I would display pretty china in a pine hutch lined with the sheet material.

SHERATON

Furniture of a graceful design created by Thomas Sheraton during the late 1700s. I love Sheraton furniture, and I love many of its characteristics. Sheraton is best known for creating ingenious pieces for unusual purposes. He used a lot of satinwood for inlays, generally with mahogany, and he often decorated his furniture with very light and delicate painted designs. He loved wreath and urn designs, and he often used lyre designs on his chair backs.

If you want a graceful dining room, try this scheme. Paint the walls a delicate pale yellow and make the trim white. Use a Sheraton sideboard with convex corners, and hang a handsome mirror or an ancestral portrait above it. Around a long rectangular mahogany table, use lyre-back Sheraton chairs. Upholster the seats in an apricot and lemon-yellow stripe. Decorate the wood stained floor with an oriental rug, and at the windows, what about apricot velvet draperies and valances lined in yellow?

SHINE

A decorative element that adds life to a room. Whether your room is traditional or contemporary, it can benefit from shine. These days shine comes in so many exciting forms: foil papers for walls, finishes for floors and furniture, chrome for accents, accessories, ta-

bles. And do you know about the great revival of polished steel furniture with its muted shine?

If your living room needs a pick-me-up, try shine. Strip the wood floor, stain it deep ebony, and keep it shining with regular applications of paste or liquid wax and frequent vacuuming (a dirt build-up scratches and dulls floors). Use a wallcovering of shiny tortoise brown patent vinyl. Against that dark background, try the drama of a soft sofa slipcovered in off-white and crowded with toss cushions in prints of wine red, poppy red, ebony, chocolate and butterscotch. Choose one of those prints and use it for upholstery on club chairs. Occasional chairs can be upholstered in poppy-red patent vinyl. For lamps, go shine again—choose brass-trimmed polished steel ones on end tables that have been lacquered poppy red.

Remember, a little shine goes a long way. A big brass bowl, a gold-framed mirror, a collection of shimmery silver-framed photos on an end table may be all the shine you need or want. Just make sure there's shine somewhere in every room of the house.

SHUTTERS

An attractive window treatment indoors and out. Shutters, so decorative and practical, come in many forms—louver, plank, filigree or trellis—and can be painted any color of the rainbow. And they don't need all the washing and rehanging that curtains do. A pair of wood-stained louvers at the family-room window can give a cozy country feeling. White shutters with applied gold moldings lend a formal French elegance to the entrance to your living room. The perfect window treatment for a French bedroom could be wood-framed shutters with shirred fabric inserts, perhaps in a floral print to match the bedspread.

Shutters can be used in many different ways, too. Friends of mine used old door shut-

142

Shutters at window

ters to divide the dining room and living room. Other friends used a vinyl wallcovering of louver shutters in their Florida room with white wicker lanai furniture and an apple-green shag carpet.

I use shutters architecturally to widen narrow windows and doorways. Try widening narrow doorways and windows in a kitchen with shutters lacquered bright blue. Paint the cabinets royal blue, too, and choose a rich mustard gold for countertops and wood trim. Use a vinyl wallcovering in a Spanish-tile pattern of blues, gold and white.

SKIRT

One of the prettiest ways I know to finish a table, a chair or a bed. I love the soft look of

skirts for bedrooms, living rooms, family rooms and even kitchens. There's nothing prettier in a kitchen than a breakfast-nook table skirted in an attractive cotton fabric. To keep that skirt fresh, use a short overcloth or place mats at mealtimes. A kitchen I designed recently featured a chocolate-brown and orange-peel color scheme. The breakfast nook's table was skirted in a cheery orange-and-white check, and the practical overcloth was chocolate-brown linen. For a different look, I used small upholstered chairs skirted and covered in the orange-and-white check around the table. I covered the floor and walls with durable sisal matting in a warm, neutral beige. Cupboard doors, ceiling and countertops were the glowing orange-peel tone. For punch, I added fresh touches of leafy green—green lacquered shutters at windows, green plants in natural wicker baskets and green accessories.

Skirts are a natural in bedrooms, too. Skirt a bed in a pastel floral cotton of apricot, raspberry and lime green on a sky-blue background. For bedspread, use quilted apricot glazed chintz. Use the floral fabric on a skirted night table. And if you have room, a dainty slipper chair upholstered and skirted in the quilted apricot cotton would be a pretty touch. Walls can be sky blue, trimmed in white. The carpet can be grass green, and white sheer draperies would be my choice.

Skirted table

SLANT-FRONT DESK

A desk with an angled top that opens into a flat writing surface. Every home needs a desk for letter-writing, homework or business. In small rooms, I like a slant-front desk because it takes up less room than a conventional desk. Most slant-front desks have lots of pigeonholes, so they're easy to keep tidy. When unexpected company arrives, desk clutter is easily camouflaged with a flip up of the slant-front—a bonus for people in one-room apartments.

SLEIGH BED

The American version of the Empire-style scroll bed. It is a low, flat bed, with a scroll-shaped arm at both ends. For the dramatic yet charming look in the guest room, why not purchase a sleigh bed? I've never known a person who disliked sleeping in the sleigh. One thing of importance to note: most antique sleigh beds are sized to house only a 3'0''-wide mattress. Our normal twin is 3'3'' wide. If you buy a sleigh, you'll need the not-so-wide mattress for it.

SLIPCOVERS

They give a warm-weather lift to your room while protecting your upholstery. Whether you make slipcovers yourself or have them custom-made, fit is the important word. Even the most beautiful slipcover fabric will look terrible if it's hanging in baggy wrinkles. Choosing the right fabric is important. Stick to firm, closely woven fabrics that will hold their shape, and avoid slippery fabrics like silk that will slither and slide and spoil the fit.

In spring, bring a wintry living room to life. Use slipcovers made of a light and bright fabric, perhaps a geometric patchwork print. Take down the heavy draperies, and replace them with simple matchstick roller blinds in canary yellow. Above the blinds, hang a valance of the patchwork print.

SPATTER

A cheerful, random pattern that even the "all thumbs" do-it-yourselfer can create. I have personally spatter-painted many floors and walls in my day, and you don't have to be a Jackson Pollock to do it. Simply paint your floor or wall the background color of your choice, choose one or two colors to spatter, dip your brush and shake. What a great project this is for a child (supervised, of course) to undertake for the floor of his own room. The spatter look, as you can imagine, is a great soil-hider for children's rooms, kitchens or any heavy-traffic area of your home.

The spatter look is so good-looking that wallcovering and fabric manufacturers have made it their own. I've seen spatter-print fabrics and wallcoverings, and these days you can accessorize a spatter-decorated room with spatterware pottery.

STAND

A great display spot for a plant, a book or a globe. I love stands—plant stands, music stands, tray stands, dictionary stands, globe stands—and use them frequently in my work. They're small enough to fit into those empty corners when nothing else will. And I like their portability: When you're tired of a stand in one room, there's always a spot for it somewhere else.

With the popularity of house plants these days, no home should be without a plant stand—an elegant English mahogany one, or ornate wicker or Victorian oak. Use one in a dark entryway and keep the plants thriving under artificial light. Or brighten a dark corner of the bedroom or living room with a fern or trailing plant on a stand.

A stand doesn't have to sit on the floor. One of my favorites is the tabletop bookstand in wood, metal or clear acrylic. If you love books, show off a favorite illustrated volume by placing it on a bookstand. In the kitchen,

Stands

why not keep a colorfully illustrated cookbook open and on display in a protective, clear acrylic bookstand?

Wooden tray stands can come in mighty handy. Why not paint one with bright-red semigloss enamel? Place the stand in a dining room and top it with a shiny brass Indian tray. This can become your family bar or tea center.

STEEL FURNITURE

A look associated with two decorative styles—French Directoire and contemporary. Did you know that some of the most beautiful pieces of polished steel furniture around are antiques of French origin? They were made during the Directoire period and look best, in my opinion, in French settings. I love French country sleigh beds of steel in particular. As for contemporary steel furniture, the glass-and-steel look for occasional tables is a classic already. I prefer the soft look of brushed steel to the highly polished look of chrome-finished steel.

STEP TABLE

An end table with two levels. English step tables with leather tops are popular with me in my decorating. I like to use an English step table at one end of the sofa and a skirted table or a vitrine table at the other. The step table also makes a very practical bedside table.

STOOLS

The littlest member of the furniture family. The stool can make a big decorating statement, especially in today's less-than-generous living quarters. I like to keep three fully upholstered square stools under a long Parsons table; when company comes, they can be pulled out to provide extra seating.

Stools can also be a touch of luxury in an otherwise modest room. If you're an antique-lover who can't afford to buy large pieces, why not use two real antique footstools with a pair of reproduction wing chairs? You can't afford to upholster your sofa or chair with that eye-catching, thirty-dollar-a-yard fabric, but I bet you could upholster a small stool with it. Or perhaps you love a certain wild, way-out color or print that you wouldn't dare use on a grand scale. Use it on a stool to provide a punchy accent.

STORAGE

A perennial decorating challenge. My solution for almost any storage problem is the stackable storage unit. They snap together, bolt together or simply stack, require no installation and can be moved from room to room. There are plastic cubes with handholds on the ends for easy transport, and there are solid cubes in wood or attractive laminate finishes. There are new skinny rectangular stackables for records and oversized books, stackable drawers, stackable wine racks, even stackable desk units. To make a colorful desk for a teenager's room, use two sets of stackable

Storage units

drawers as supports for a plywood door painted a coordinated color.

Paint is the secret behind turning blah office storage units into bright and useful accents for the home. Old two-drawer filing cabinets can be prettied up with a coat of paint and used as bedside tables in a teenager's room. Bolt-together steel shelf units come to life with a coat of yellow, red, green or blue paint. Put one in your hallway to hold books, or in your family room for the television set and for your collection of objects d'art.

STRIÉ

A wavy or streaked-looking fabric made by using threads of different tones. Also a painted wall finish that is the decorating rage of the Seventies. A lovely woven pink strié fabric could be your choice for the upholstery on your powder-room stool. The strié fabric will most likely have streaks of different color pinks in the finished goods.

If pink strié is the look you select for walls, your painter will most likely first paint your walls a deeper pink shade than the desired color. After it has dried, your painter will cover the walls with a lighter pink paint or with white. While wet, he will start brushing over or combing out the wet light pink or wet white, so the background coat of deep pink will begin to show again. This creates the strié look.

SURPRISE

The difference between a "so-so" room and a "so-super" room. The next time you see a room done by a decorator, look closely, and I bet you'll find an element of surprise somewhere—in the accessories, the colors or the mix of styles. Very often this surprise involves using objects, fabrics or colors in unexpected ways—filling a shiny copper cooking pot with flowers for a casual centerpiece, upholstering a contemporary molded acrylic chair with a scrap of antique patchwork, putting a top on an old barrel and using it as an end table. Create surprise with color. Try shiny eggplant walls in a half bath, terra-cotta walls in a country kitchen, a floor painted white and topped with colorful rag rugs.

In your bedroom reverse the usual look of light walls with a dark spread. Instead, paint your walls surprising coral red. Paint trim and ceiling creamy ivory and choose a creamy ivory quilted spread. Carpet can be thick champagne beige shag. For window drama, choose a large-scale print of coral-red roses with green leaves on a cream background. Hang those draperies from poles painted ivory.

SWATCH

A small sample of fabric or paper that shows you how it looks and feels. I do not use swatches of material when selecting patterns for drapery or upholstry. A swatch of a large repeating pattern will never show you what you are getting. When you want to see how a pattern will look on your sofa or at your windows, request a large memo sample. Swatches should be used for solid colors only.

T

TAILORED LOOK

A decorating style inspired by fine fashions. While you're outfitting yourself with the new tailored fashions, what about giving your home a touch of the same? I can think of so many tailored touches for the home: tailored skirts for sofas and chairs, simple tailored draperies, upholstery of pinstripes, hound's tooth or small plaids.

The tailored look is right at home in the bedroom, paticularly when that bedroom doubles as a home office. Let's imagine a scheme of gray flannel and soft pink; I'll start with walls papered in a tailored plaid of soft pink and white. Paint trim and ceiling white.

For fitted bedspread and draperies, my choice would be lightweight gray flannel. The bedspread should go right to the floor and should have neat inverted pleats at the corners. On the floor I would lay a carpet of soft dove gray, and for a touch of softness, I would drop a furry white bedside rug over the carpet. And wouldn't bedside lamps of pewter, shaded in white, complete the picture beautifully?

Tailored look

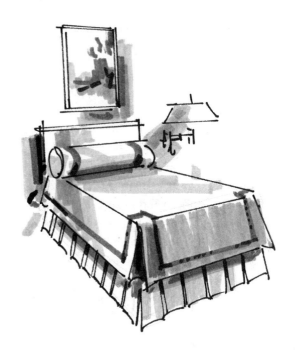

TAUPE

One of the great color mixers. Taupe as a mixer can't be beat. Try it with greens, pinks, reds, blues—there isn't a color that doesn't blend with taupe. I love using it with bright colors in room schemes.

A hotel I once visited in the Caribbean had all the furniture lacquered taupe and highlighted with pulls and trim of sparkling white. Walls were fresh white. For color, the draperies and a bedskirt were made from a tropical bird and flower print of hot pink, sunny yellow, sharp green and sky blue on a taupe background. The bedspread was white, welted with the print, and the ruffled pillow shams were of the colorful cotton, too.

TENTED CEILING

Cloth draped up to a ceiling, creating a tented effect. In the mid-1960s I went tent crazy. I tented foyers, dining rooms, kitchens—just about every room in the house, including the bath.

My favorite tented room was a foyer. Its ceiling was covered with lemon and lime striped fabric. The tent valance was lime green, trimmed in yellow. The walls were yellow, above a white dado, and the floor was covered with black and white vinyl square tiles. A crystal chandelier hung from the center of the ceiling tent, with all bulbs being covered with white opaque shades.

TERRA-COTTA

A rich reddish-brown color that will warm any interior. There are many ways to add a dash of terra-cotta to your home. A terra-cotta entryway provides a warm welcome for guests. Terra-cotta walls are a wonderful backdrop for any kind of artwork. In the living room, you can give new life to a faded green-and-gold scheme by papering the walls in a jagged stripe of terra-cotta, creamy ivory and grass green. Cover your occasional chair seats in nubby terra-cotta cotton and make throw pillows with the additional yardage.

And don't forget the potential of real terra-cotta tile. It can be used almost anywhere—in dining rooms, family rooms, living rooms and even in bedrooms. A sleek, up-to-date version of a Mediterranean bedroom might start with terra-cotta tiles on the floor. Of course you'll want fluffy carpets at bedside for comfort. Paint walls pure white, using a rough sand paint. Top the bed with a striped spread of peach and off-white cotton, and hang matching draperies at the windows. At bedsides, chunky terra-cotta lamps with ivory parchment shades would be my choice.

TERRY CLOTH

These days, it means more than just towels. Terry cloth in colors, prints, stripes and textures is being seen in every room of the house—particularly when that house is by the sea or near a lake. Friends of mine have terry cloth in tropical colors covering the seats of wicker furniture at their seaside home. The wicker is painted sparkling white, and the seat pads are solid hot pink, lemon yellow and grass green. Rugged board walls have been stained white, and the floor is white easy-care vinyl brick. Curtains of sailcloth are bright grass green. For extra seating my friends keep plenty of terry-cloth cushions around in the green, pink and yellow tones. And all covers zip off for quick trips to the washing machine.

TEXTURE

Smoothness and roughness that can make a big decorating difference. Interesting textures in fabrics, carpets, wallcoverings and vinyls come in so many easy-to-use forms these days. For walls, there are stucco, wallboard, sand paint, grass cloths, cork, suede cloths and flocking. For floors, there are carpets of velvety plushes, ribbed corduroy, rugged hand-woven looks, smooth indoor-outdoor materials and nubby sisal matting. Upholstery fabrics today offer a great range of terrific textures, including the new rustic handwoven looks.

A living room I decorated recently is a good example. In that room I played the sheen of lacquer against the roughness of Berber wool carpeting and suede cloth and nubby cotton upholstery. Walls were painted shiny espresso brown with trim and ceiling of pale ivory. For sofa upholstery I chose rugged suede cloth in a fawn beige. Chairs were slip-covered in rough white Haitian cotton, and the same cotton was used for draperies. Smooth-as-glass sand-beige lacquer was featured on occasional tables. Green plants were housed in rough woven baskets in shades ranging from nut brown to pale straw. The room, you will note, has no bright color in it. Instead, eye appeal comes from the range of textures used.

TICKING-STRIPE

A mattress-cover stripe that has graduated into the world of decorative fabrics and wallcoverings. I have seen ticking-stripe walls in elegant bedrooms and ticking-stripe upholstery used lavishly in sitting rooms. A ticking-stripe in black and white makes elegant summer slipcovers even for a room that's decorated with costly antiques. And it mixes easily with florals, geometrics, checks and plaids.

Ticking-stripe wallcovering

Ticking-stripes can give a sporty look to a boy's room. Use a classic blue-and-white ticking-stripe wallcovering and faded denim for bedspreads. The carpet can be bright red. The same blue-and-white ticking-stripe walls could also be the basis for a pretty master bedroom with a blue, pink, yellow and white floral print for ruffled spread and draperies and a plush cosmos pink carpet underfoot. In either room, window shades laminated with blue-and-white ticking-stripe fabric would be a perfect touch.

TIE-DYE

A way to create abstract designs by tying a fabric before dyeing it. Tie-dye had its heyday in the 1960s, but that doesn't mean the look is dead. Tie-dye is still a fun look for a teenager's room or for a weekend hideaway at the beach or in the woods. And it's easy to do. A friend of mine redecorated the living room of her beach house in tie-dye, using plain white sheets and dyes in pale sea blues and greens. Her draperies were dyed in stripes, and her slipcovers were dyed in sunbursts. The room, with its cool sky-blue walls, white ceiling and tie-dye draperies and slipcovers, was as cool as a dip in the surf!

TILE

The Spanish variety, that is. I love the look of Spanish tiles. Rooms done in hand-painted tile look so cool and inviting to me. Of course, a whole room of real handpainted tile is a luxury few of us can afford. Instead, use handpainted tiles for accents. One woman I know used yellow and terra-cotta tiles just on the windowsills of her country kitchen. Or you could tile just the small backsplash area behind the sink or stove. For a full wall or floor treatment of Spanish tiles, go vinyl. There are hundreds of beautiful tile designs in floor and wallcoverings on the market that can be used in any room of the house.

I like Spanish tile floor designs in the

Tile in a kitchen

family room with heavy Spanish-style furniture. Lay a vinyl floor in a pale-blue, lemon-yellow and white tile pattern.Upholster your Spanish-style furniture in a happy yellow cotton duck. Paint the walls pale blue, and stain woodwork with a dark oak stain. On end tables, place terra-cotta lamps with sunny yellow opaque painted shades. At your windows, hang Roman shades in a narrow blue-and-yellow vertical stripe. And be sure to use cactus plants and geraniums in decorative terra-cotta planters as accessories.

TOAST

A color for all seasons. A toast scheme in the living room is a wise idea because it can be adapted to look just right for any season. Start by painting living-room walls creamy white. For the floor, try a toast-colored, deep shag carpet. Upholster twin love seats in toast. Occasional chairs can be natural wicker, and the tables can be either natural wicker or white lacquered wood. In winter, pile toss pillows of chocolate, emerald green, russet, tomato red and rich autumn gold on the love seats. Seat pads on wicker chairs can be emerald green. For winter draperies, go toast in a basket-weave fabric hung over white sheers. When warm weather comes, take down those toast draperies and replace them with pure white, or, if practical, let the white sheers hang alone. Zip on summery toss pillow covers of palest lavender, celadon green, soft lemon yellow, apple green and white. Chair seat pads can be changed to lavender, welted in apple green.

Add a cool-looking throw rug of white over that toast carpet. For all-season lamps, brass with white linen shades would be my choice.

TOILE DE JOUY

That pretty scenic design depicting French aristocrats and peasants at work and play.

The design originally came in only four colors—red, green, blue or eggplant—all on a cream background. Today, the choice of colors is wider, and there are pure white backgrounds available in addition to the more traditional cream. I like red-and-cream toile wallpaper in a formal dining room above a wood-paneled dado. It's a super look with tie-back draperies of a matching toile fabric. On a polished wood floor, under a mahogany or walnut dining-room table and chairs, lay an

Aubusson-type area rug in reds, pinks and greens on a creamy background. Cover the seats of dining chairs in red cotton moire. Leave your dining table uncovered so the warm polished wood shows. And make sure you include a centerpiece of red-and-white blooms and green ferns in a silver bowl.

Toile is for traditionalists, but that doesn't mean it can't work with contemporary furnishings. For example, you could do the same dining room in a less formal vein and still use the toile for walls and draperies. I would choose a white Parsons table. For chairs, I would use the high-backed French country type. Paint the exposed arms and legs with bright Chinese-red lacquer, and upholster the seats and backs in red-and-white toile. Paint the paneled dado white and carpet in emerald green.

Toile de Jouy room

151

TORTOISE

A warm, sophisticated look for walls, furniture and accessories. Real tortoise-shell ornaments are no longer being made—we don't want the tortoise to become extinct. But tortoise fans needn't deprive themselves. Thanks to modern technology and skilled artisans, the tortoise-shell look will never be extinct. And there are still many beautiful and valuable antique tortoise-shell ornaments around.

You can have as much of the tortoise look as you want, thanks to man-made reproductions of this natural wonder. Did you know that manufacturers make tortoise-design wall-coverings of vinyl? For tortoise lovers, here's a look that's sure to please. Cover walls with tortoise vinyl wallcovering. Paint woodwork and doors white, and finish the ceiling in reflective gold-leaf paint. Hang tangy tomato-red draperies and valances over bronze-tone or silvery small-slat venetian blinds. For sofa upholstery, choose a print of beige, pale blue and white on a tomato-red background. Club chairs can be covered in a beige-and-champagne textured fabric. Shiny brass lamps on black-lacquered end tables would be my choice. And be sure to throw a few tomato-red toss pillows on that sofa.

TRIM

One of the little decorating details that makes a big difference. Trim for draperies, slipcovers and even papered or fabric-covered walls should never be ignored. The right trim can create a mood, while the wrong trim can ruin all other decorating efforts. In a nautical room, for instance, white rope welt trim on slipcovers and draperies is a very important touch. In a charming French bedroom, how important that wide band of embroidered ribbon on draperies is. And how handsome a band of solid-color tape can look on plain slipcovers! Choosing the right trim should be done with as much care as choosing furniture, lamps and fabrics.

TROMPE L'OEIL

French words for *deceive the eye*. Wall murals with objects painted to look as real as possible. I once saw a library filled with book-covered walls. Upon closer examination I discovered that the books on the walls were actually a mural. A super *trompe l'oeil* painter is hard to find, but super *trompe l'oeil* murals are readily available on the market. If you want a fool-the-eye decoration in your entry foyer or library or wherever, consider *trompe l'oeil* murals.

TROPICAL LOOK

A cool-as-a-breeze look that can work in any clime. Bring those sunny tropics into your home through your decorating. To me, the tropics mean lush vegetation. So for tropical decorating, lots and lots of live green plants are a must—and no plastic imitations, please. Put those green plants into tropical containers: wicker, raffia or terra-cotta. The tropics mean fresh, natural colors—sea and sky blue, palm green, sunshine yellow, sparkling sand, bougainvillea scarlet and, of course, splashes of white everywhere. The tropics also mean louvers for windows and doors—a convenient and pretty way to keep out sun and let in soft tropical breezes. And the tropics wouldn't be the tropics without airy wicker furniture.

TRUNK

A useful and decorative accessory for the home. Antique trunks, modern trunks, wicker trunks, miniature trunks—they're all making the decorating scene in a big way because there are so many ways to use them. Trunk coffee tables are popular in today's homes. There is even a trunk-style table that has pull-out drawers. And have you seen the beautiful miniature brass trunks that make super tabletop accessories? I saw some recently used as a centerpiece; the lids were open, and the trunks were filled with loose bouquets of lilies,

Tropical look

daisies and baby's breath. Or how about a trunk to sit on? Slip a lacquered metal trunk under the window and top it with a slip-covered foam cushion for an instant window seat. To give the window seat a built-in look, you can flank it with built-in or stacking book-cases.

TUXEDO SOFA

A sofa classic. With its simple high back and arms, the squared-off Tuxedo sofa will never go out of style and can change its look as your tastes change. I have known Tuxedo owners to switch gracefully from an Early American look to a French Provincial look. In the Early American scheme, the Tuxedo might be upholstered in wide-wale cordoury. To make the switch to French Provincial choose

Tuxedo sofa

beige-and-white toile slipcovers, and cover the walls with the same design. If there's a fire-place in the room, try to find a French-style wood mantelpiece. At windows, wood shutters under tie-back toile draperies would be the perfect touch.

153

U

UPHOLSTERED FURNITURE

Make sure you buy the best. Unfortunately, the things that literally make or break an upholstered piece—the frame, the springs, the padding and the webbing—are all hidden. Short of cutting the upholstery open and examining the construction, the only way you can be sure you're making a good choice is to shop in a reputable store and ask the right questions of the salesman.

Look for a frame of good, kiln-dried hardwood such as birch or hard maple. Make sure the piece you choose is joined with dowels, pegs or wood screws—never with nails. Look for steel coil springs; poor-quality furniture often has wooden slats instead of springs.

If your budget does not allow the purchase of quality upholstered furniture, wait until you can save enough to buy it. If you must have a sofa or chairs right away, look into the new molded urethane models. Because there's no complicated construction involved, they cost less than traditional upholstered pieces.

UPHOLSTERED LOOK

It's climbing the walls! The soft look of upholstery is no longer confined to furniture. It is also being seen on walls, tables, chests of drawers and even curtain poles. And it is finding its way onto the legs of chairs, sofas and ottomans, giving upholstered furniture a softer look.

Upholstery for tables or chests works best with simple straight-edged pieces such as Parsons tables. The fabric—a soft, slightly stretchy one is best—can be attached directly to the furniture or can be stretched over a soft underlining. In your living room, try upholstering a console table in a fabric to match your draperies. And when your club chairs and sofa come up for reupholstering, tell the man you want him to put on upholstered bun feet.

A bedroom I saw recently was softly pulled together with upholstery on furniture and curtain poles. The fabric used was a delicate hydrangea-blue floral print with green foliage on a white background. It was applied with wallpaper paste to two inexpensive dress-

ers, and it was also used for floor-length draperies hung on white rings from a wooden pole
wrapped in the fabric. Walls were painted
hydrangea blue with white trim and ceiling.
The carpet was fern-green shag. The bedspread was of the same print and was comple-
mented by a lacy white eyelet bed skirt and a
scattering of eyelet-edged baby pillows. A
penny-bright brass headboard and two brass
wall sconces added twinkling warmth to this
soft, soft upholstered room.

USED FURNITURE

Forget it! Don't try to furnish your house
with pieces from a garage sale. The pieces
won't fit and the look will never be satisfying
to your eye. I've been to a lot of garage sales
and I've never found anything of real style or
value yet. (I'm still looking, however.)

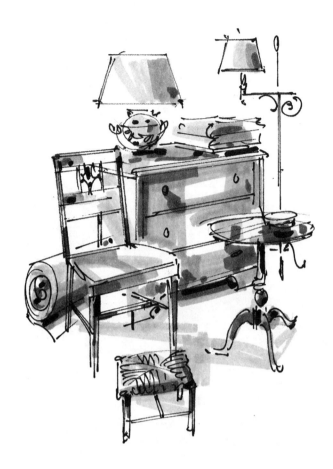

Typical used furniture

156

V

VELVET

An elegant pile fabric that's all over the decorating market. Velvet is probably one of America's favorite fabrics, but it is not an all-purpose fabric. It is appropriate in all elegant and Victorian rooms, but it is totally inappropriate in most casual, natural-look or country rooms. Most American homes are not lavish enough to warrant the use of many of the ornate cut-velvet fabrics on the market. I do, however, admire the velvets cut in simple stripes or geometrics, and when velvet is appropriate, it can be used everywhere.

Here's how a friend of mine did her living room the velvet way. Walls are covered in rich burgundy cut velvet (the cut design is a simple one of inch-wide stripes). What a backdrop those walls are for a celery-green velvet sofa, a rich mahogany grand piano and a jewel-tone oriental rug! Draperies are also burgundy velvet, and there is a wing chair covered in a Persian fabric of burgundy, celery green, rich blue and cream. Lamps on mahogany end tables are antique Chinese jars in shades of green and pink on a cream ground. The shades are white pleated silk.

VENEER

A thin layer of fine wood used to finish and decorate wood furniture. Veneers are very much a part of the great world of wood furniture. When buying wood furniture, don't think that a veneered piece is cheap or of poor quality. It doesn't have to be and often isn't. Because of what is commonly called "a sandwiched construction," veneered furniture doesn't warp, and with veneers you can get so many different grains. When buying veneered furniture, remember to look for good construction. Look at the joints on a chest of drawers or dining table. The joints are what gives strength, and they should be tight and fit securely without the use of plastic filler. When a joint is glued haphazardly, you can be certain the piece of furniture is not made well at all.

VENETIAN BLINDS

They're better than ever! Remember when venetian blinds were so ugly you wanted to hide them? Today, due to the revolution in the colors and designs of blinds, they are so beautiful they're being used as room dividers,

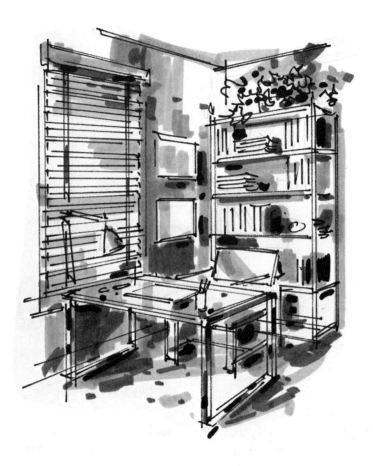

Venetian blinds

as camouflage for unattractive storage areas and as elements in supergraphics. I've seen blinds in plum, hot pink, lemon yellow and scores of other exciting shades, as well as in gold, brass and aluminum finishes.

And have you seen those great gingham-check blinds? Try yellow ones in a bathroom with yellow tiles, a thick white carpet underfoot and walls and ceiling covered in a floral print of cornflower blue, apricot, lemon and petal pink on a white ground. Towels can be grass green and cornflower blue, and the shower curtain can be yellow gingham.

If you're an antiques fan, look for handsome old-fashioned wood blinds to go in your pretty period rooms. One of my favorite living rooms was decorated in the English manner with natural wood blinds at all the windows. Rich tie-back draperies of heavy cranberry silk were hung over the blinds. The carpet was cranberry, topped with oriental scatter rugs in

shades of cranberry, blue and gold. The two Chesterfield sofas were upholstered in brown leather, and wing chairs were covered in a damask of cerulean blue and cranberry tapestry. The walls were wood-paneled.

VERTICAL FURNITURE

An old look in furniture that is being revived to suit today's lifestyle. As rooms get smaller, many people are turning to vertical furniture as a storage solution. Why use a row of long, low bookcases when a ceiling-high wall unit will hold twice as much? Why store your wardrobe in a long, low chest of drawers when you can store as much in a single armoire that uses only half the floor space? And vertical pieces have another plus: They break up the long, boring boxiness that is a feature of most modern homes.

I'm all in favor of using an armoire, hutch

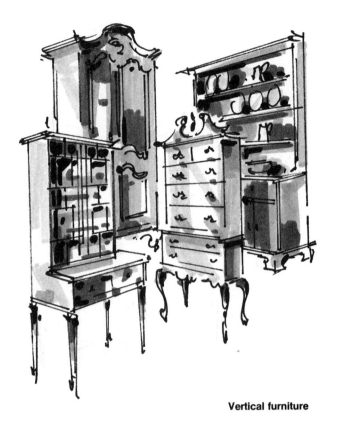

Vertical furniture

Victorian look

or other dramatic vertical piece as a living-room focal point. If it's a hutch you choose, use the shelves above for display and the lower, closed portion for storage. If you choose one with a rich wood finish, try planning a blue-and-white scheme around it. Paint walls a soft faded denim blue, and use a carpet of the same color with an off-white stripe in it. For sofa upholstery and draperies, a batik in shades of blue and white would be my choice. Complete the blue-and-white scheme by upholstering two wood-framed bergère chairs in a small-scale plaid of navy, egg-yolk yellow and white.

VICTORIAN

An ornate, heavy look that flourished under England's Queen Victoria. The Victorian look is quite alive and well. People are getting the message that the look is not as straight-laced and stuffy as the word "Victorian" implies. The Victorians were fasci-

nated by the exotic Ottoman empire, and no Victorian home was complete without a pasha-style divan heaped with cushions and heavily draped with lush fabrics. They loved luxurious velvets and brocades, and they often used those fabrics or paper equivalents on their walls.

All that velvet and brocade made those Victorian dwellings dark, not in keeping with the taste of today. But that doesn't mean the Victorian look has no place in today's homes—it does, if modified appropriately. For instance, you could use your Victorian oak dining chairs and table in a dramatic all-white scheme—sparkling white walls, white draperies hung over wooden shutters, white chair pads and bare wood floor. Or you could lighten your Victoriana by painting the furniture itself. I did that once with a Victorian armoire; the outside was given a coat of white paint and the inside was finished with yellow and white gingham-checked fabric. The armoire became the focal point of a bedroom.

159

W

WALL GROUPINGS

Designs for walls, including framed pictures. A kitchen wall grouping can be created from almost any collection of objects—colorful baskets, fiber place mats, wooden spoons, rolling pins, cutting boards and old cookie molds. On a white dining-room wall, group a collection of colorful plates. You can group a collection of tiny framed mirrors on a bathroom wall. Or you can make a grouping of children's art and family photographs.

WALLPAPER

The greatest decorating tool in the world. Wallpaper goes back to the late sixteenth and early seventeenth centuries in France, and it served as a very inexpensive substitute for real brocades and damasks. In the eighteenth century block printed wallpapers were available to match all the pretty voiles of the time. Today canvas- and paper-backed wallcoverings are the rage with decorators. I love rooms covered with beautiful floral print or striped wallcoverings.

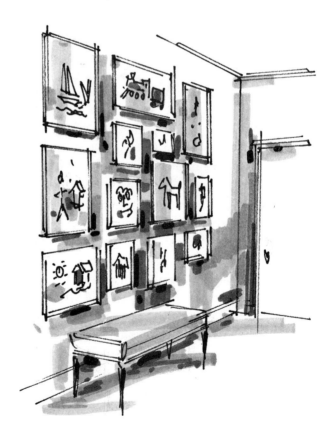

Wall grouping

161

WARM LOOK

A decorating mood created with subtler and softer colors of the sunset. Would you like to create a warm living room? Paint your walls soft cantaloupe and all trim off-white. For carpeting, choose a trellis design of yellow on melon. Select a summery print for your sofa of reds, melons, yellows and beiges on an off-white background. For club-chair upholstery, a yellow and beige tweed would be my choice. Draperies can match the sofa fabric, and they should be lined in yellow. Furniture can be a mix of warm fruitwoods, and if you are planning on a skirted table anywhere in the room its fabric might be a large cantaloupe and beige geometric check.

WATERMELON

Luscious, juicy and terrific—for decorating as well as for eating. Use that succulent watermelon pink on anything, but remember that a little watermelon goes a long way. Use it sparingly in your decorating, and mix it with other colors—cool leafy green, sky blue and lots of summer white. Watermelon also goes well with light natural wood and with wicker.

For a summery family room start with walls of rich watermelon pink. Paint all the wood trim, doors and ceiling pure white. Upholster two love seats in white sailcloth and accent them with lots of toss pillows in a colorful Indian print fabric of watermelon pink, mandarin orange, watermelon-rind green, white and ebony. Use the same print for a skirted end table. For chairs, how about one or two old oak rockers, bleached to a light shade? At the windows, try matchstick roller blinds in a natural finish, and for draperies use white sailcloth under a valance of the Indian print. And underfoot use a sisal carpet in the lightest natural shade you can find.

WELSH DRESSER

A side table with cupboards and drawers

Welsh dresser

on the bottom and shelves up top. On that set-back upper section of your Welsh dresser, may I suggest displaying a collection of your favorite china or pewter?

I have seen Welsh dressers used in rooms other than the dining room. If your Welsh dresser is used in the library, the upper section may be the space for displaying your collections. A friend of mine uses a Welsh dresser in her bedroom; the top shelves are used for displaying photographs of family and friends.

WESTERN LOOK

The soft, natural look of the desert and the plains. Cactus, American Indian baskets and geometric prints, desert colors, adobe, stucco and bleached wood are part of the Western look, and I'm all for it, provided those Western influences are used sparingly.

Here's my idea of a beautiful bedroom where Western influences are strong but subtle. The walls are off-white stucco, and all trim is natural bleached wood. The floor is covered with pale beige sisal matting, topped with an

Western look

Indian rug in shades of beige and brown. The bedspread is cotton with stripes of pale coral, cactus green, sky blue and beige, and all the furniture is bleached pine. Woven baskets filled with cacti are perfect accessories.

WHITE

You can't go wrong with white! White is a great brightener for dark rooms, and white can make small rooms look larger. White is restful, too, so it's ideal for bedrooms, family rooms and living rooms. And white goes with all looks.

Today's miracle products make a white room as practical as can be. Try this living-room scheme and you'll see what I mean. Paint walls and trim white, using washable oil-based paint. Paint floor white, too, with scrub-bable Polyurethane paint, and lay a fluffy white area rug of machine-washable fake fur over it. For sofa upholstery, how about white vinyl that washes clean with a sponge? The sofa should have a frame of warm, honey-tone wood, and the end tables can be cubes of that same wood. End-table lamps can be gleaming brass. Upholster a club chair in nubby white cotton. For your second chair, how about an old-fashioned bentwood-and-cane rocker? At windows, hang natural bamboo roller blinds and place some live green plants there, too. If you want some color, put up a few wall posters and paintings, and use toss cushions of your favorite colors on the sofa.

WICKER

Don't limit it to the porch! Wicker is versatile. It can be painted white and covered with a colorful bird-and-flower print for a sum-

163

Wicker furniture

mery look. It can also be painted any color, stained honey or ebony or left in its natural state. It can be mixed with antiques in an elegant setting or with country furniture in a converted barn or cottage.

In an Early American family room where an extra chair or two is needed, go wicker. Stain the chair frames a warm honey tone and cover the seats with inexpensive green-and-white gingham. Paint walls white, using stucco paint. The carpet can be rich forest green. Upholster your Early American sofa in a floral print of forest green, burgundy and tomato red. Hang crisp green-and-white gingham café curtains at windows. If a wall unit is needed, consider wicker in natural or stained a rich honey tone.

WINDOWS

Make yours a decorating asset. Almost everybody has trouble decorating windows.

One problem is the small horizontal clerestory window that is featured in so many ranch houses. I favor the solution I once saw in a home where the owner hung long, narrow panes of stained glass from the ceiling in front of her windows for a pretty effect. The wide picture window is another decorating problem. If there's a panoramic view beyond the window, that is all the decoration you need. To frame the view you might want to install a fabric-covered frame or trellis frame around the window. And what about the glass patio door? Please don't swathe it in yards and yards of heavy fabric unless your home is an extremely formal one. You can hang plants in pretty containers in front of it. You can hang floor-length café curtains across its bottom half. If privacy is not required, leave the glass bare and decorate the wall around your door. If a viewless window in the city is your problem, screen it off, using an openwork screen of some kind—lattice, cane or carved wood.

164

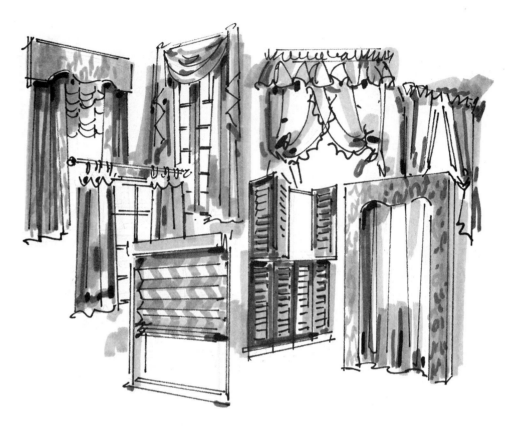

Ways to decorate windows

WINDSOR CHAIR

An English and later American country chair. I love the country look of Windsor chairs. I might use them in a contemporary white dining room around an emerald-green Parsons table or a glass-and-steel table. Underfoot, I picture a thick geometric patterned Moroccan rug in brilliant red, orange and green tones over a polished wood floor. For added punch, I would hang colorful paintings on the walls. Chair pads and floor-length draperies can be made from chevron-patterned emerald green and white cotton.

Windsor chairs

WINE

A word with many decorative meanings. Many Americans are becoming wine experts, and they are finding that there are many styles of wine racks and cabinets in which to store their bottles. There are wine racks of colorful molded plastic and of fine wood. There are protable, folding wine racks and elegant wine cabinets in period styles with thermostatically controlled interiors. There are wine-rack components to use with modular wall units.

Even without the real thing, there are many ways to decorate around the wine theme. You can paint your walls a wine color—rich burgundy, warm sherry or pale champagne beige. And I love the look of walls papered with real wine labels or with printed wine-label wallcoverings. One of my favorites comes in soft natural shades plus burgundy and hunter green. Don't you think it would look super in a family room with a beamed ceiling, sherry-colored leather sofas and a burgundy carpet?

Many do-it-yourselfers are using wine labels for decoupage. I like wine-label tabletops. Large tabletops can be protected by sheets of clear glass or acrylic, but smaller ones need only several coats of clear varnish.

WING CHAIR

A graceful addition to any room. I don't know anyone who can resist the charm and comfort of wing chairs. My favorite spot for one is by the fireside. With another chair nearby for company and a tiny table for my coffee cup, I can't think of a cozier spot.

At one time only traditional fabrics were used for upholstery—crewels, leathers, velvets, linens or chintz prints. But today I also enjoy seeing a wing chair sporting a less traditional look—white duck, chenille, African-inspired prints, batiks, patent vinyls or denim. How about a blue and white batik-covered wing chair in a family room with a blue denim-covered sofa, a warm rust-colored carpet and white walls? Or how about a red patent vinyl wing chair as a bright color accent in a girl's room done up in a posy print of red and white for walls, bedspread and curtains?

WINTERIZE

Get your home ready for the cold and indoor season. Winter, for the cold-state people, is the time to cozy-up the house. Place happy quilts on the beds. Buy a new log basket for the fireplace. Toss colorful needlepoint pillows on the sofa. Hang your warm melon dining-room draperies and valances. Bring the area rugs back to warm up the floors. Hang up the plant baskets. Do the things to your rooms that will make people want to use them!

X-BASE

Legs of a table, chair or sofa bench forming an X. The X-base glass-top table with steel legs is very popular in modern decorating. Use one in front of a modern sofa over a pretty Persian or sculptured modern geometric area rug.

My favorite X-base piece of furniture, indoors as well as outdoors, is the picnic table. If space permits, why not use one in your kitchen? The seats can be covered with bright yellow and red checkered pads, and place mats on the table can alternate between red and yellow.

X-base furniture

167

Y

YARD GOODS

Fabric sold by the yard right off the bolt. Yard goods are one of my greatest sources of decorating inspiration. Never has there been such a variety to choose from. I don't limit my yard goods shopping to upholstery fabric departments. I have discovered super yard goods in five-and-dime stores and in apparel fabric departments and shops. Men's suiting fabrics, summery dress-weight voiles and tailored cotton shirting fabrics can all be purchased in fabric shops and used in the home. And certain sheeting fabrics are now sold by the yard so that it's easier than ever to coordinate the bedroom from windows to walls to bed.

YELLOW

One of my favorite colors. Yellow is always right. Whether it is the yellow of the sun, of daffodils, of tangy lemons or of pineapple, you can mix it with any color you can think of. I love "citrus" schemes of soft lemon yellow, tangy lime and brilliant orange-peel orange. Tone the same scheme down for an elegant, traditional room. You can use a soft lemon-

Yard goods

chiffon yellow on the walls, an almost-apricot in velvet for sofa upholstery and a flamestitch of lemon, orange and lime for club chairs. Tangy green accents would be the perfect way to complete the look.

169

Z

ZEBRA

A zesty black-and-white design to use on walls, floors, upholstery. I would never advocate killing an animal for its hide, but happily we can still enjoy the look of zebra in the home. Fabric manufacturers are helping with zebra-print fabrics with both pile and flat surfaces. Wallcovering manufacturers are also featuring the zebra look. For the floor, there are zebra-look rugs that look real enough to pet! And you don't have to settle for nature's black and white (which, by the way, is still my favorite). With the fakes, you can have yellow-and-white zebra, blue-and-white zebra or any other combination.

For a bathroom with a safari look, start with zebra walls and ceiling of chocolate brown and white. Fixtures are white, and the carpet is poppy red. For towels, go chocolate brown and poppy red. Accessories—wastebasket, tissue dispenser and wall hangings—can be brown wicker. Hang a shiny brown vinyl shower curtain around the tub. If you have a window in the bathroom, make your jungle look come to life with live green plants hung from the ceiling in brown wicker baskets.

Make sure you choose plants that thrive on humidity, such as Boston ferns.

ZIGZAG

An eye-opening pattern to use everywhere. Zigzags are everywhere. Have you ever seen a zigzag floor? I created one by staining a herringbone parquet floor in alternating light and dark stripes. And since the zigzag pattern is an ancient one, it can be used with any decorating style—contemporary or traditional.

If your home is traditional, why not upholster in a zigzag print inspired by bargello work or flamestitch? Choose a pattern in soft yellows and ivory for upholstery against walls of pale lemon yellow. Stain floors rich ebony black and lay an area rug of thick lemony pile bordered in off-white. For draperies, narrow stripes of lemon, gold and white would be my choice.

Add excitement to a dull kitchen with a zigzag wallcovering. Choose a small-scale print that will fit comfortably into all of a kitchen's odd-shaped crannies. Citrus colors—lime, orange and lemon—would be pretty, es-

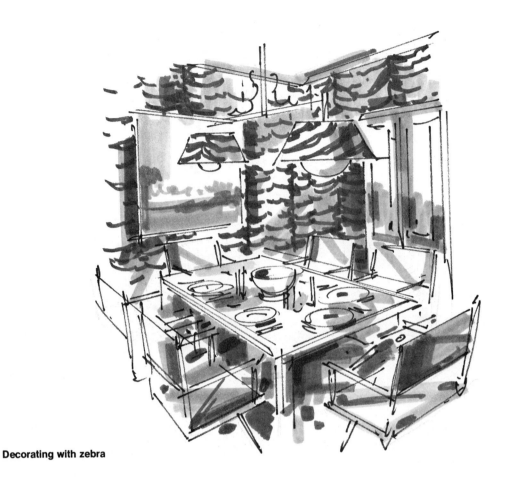

Decorating with zebra

Zigzag floor

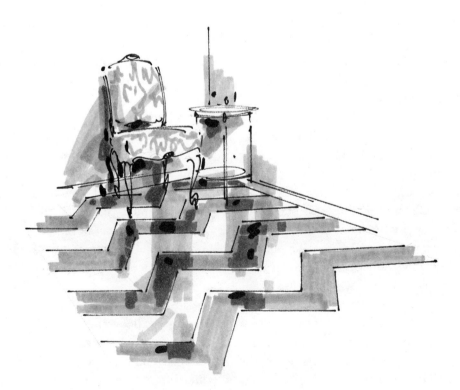

pecially if teamed with pickled-pine cabinets, lemon-yellow countertops and a floor of lemon and white vinyl tiles laid zigzag fashion.

ZINGY COLOR

One of the most effective and least expensive items in the decorator's bag of tricks. Zingy color has always been one of my trademarks as a decorator. Of course, I can and do decorate with soft colors, but even a soft color scheme can have zing. For instance, you can add zing to an all-beige room by using chocolate brown, rust and black accessories. An all-avocado-green room certainly lacks zing, but it can be helped by accents of pink, daffodil and lemon yellow along with zingy blue and purple tones.

The zingiest color of all is red, and I've seen all-red rooms that are as lovely as can be. But I don't advocate that look for everyone. It's not a good idea to paint a room red if you plan to spend many hours in it. Instead paint it white, chocolate brown, beige or blue and use the zingy red as an accent color.

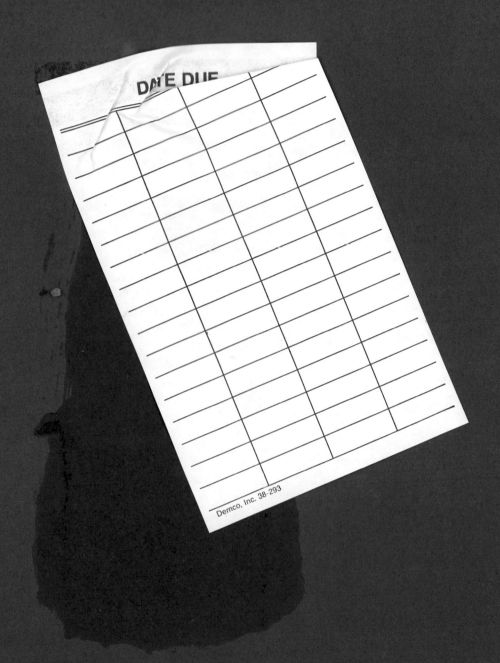

DATE DUE

Demco, Inc. 38-293